The Bible Reconsidered

A Journey from Fundamentalism
to Progressive Christianity

Paul Brynteson

Antero
PUBLISHING
Broomfield, CO

Interior Design:
Concepts Unlimited
www.ConceptsUnlimitedInc.com

ISBN-13:978-0-61587-531-6   (pbk)
ISBN-10: 0615875319
13   14   15   16   17   0 9 8 7 6 5 4 3 2 1

First Printing, 2013
Printed in the United States of America

DEDICATION

This book is dedicated to evangelical/fundamentalist Christians who have occasionally wondered whether everything they are reading in the Bible or hearing in their churches is really true. Is the Bible the Word of God? Did God really create the world in 7 days? Did a literal Adam really name all the animals? Was a rib taken from Adam to create Eve? Did God send a flood to destroy the world and save only Noah and his family? Can healing, prosperity, protection, and success be expected from God if you plant the right "seeds," give to the "right" ministries, believe the correct doctrines, make the acceptable confessions, and pray the proper prayers?

This book is dedicated to those who, when they have questioned any of the fundamentals of evangelical Christianity, have been told, "never question the scriptures," or "we don't go there," or "it's a slippery slope to ever question our basic beliefs." This book is dedicated to those who have struggled with accepting the Bible as the literal Word of God and have felt condemned or guilty because of their reservations. A 2011 Gallup survey reported that 30 percent of the USA adult population believes in the literal interpretation of the Bible.

This book is dedicated to five specific Oral Roberts University (ORU) students. In my 14 years on the faculty at ORU, I arranged student ski trips to Colorado over Spring break. While driving across Kansas, returning from one of our trips, these five students shared with me in confidence, that they were deeply troubled by the theology that permeated ORU and they were considering transferring since they were concerned about having a diploma from ORU. But, they also felt deeply guilty, conflicted, and distressed by the thought, "are we rejecting God?" Their upbringing in the church and time at ORU made it extremely difficult to confront their qualms.

This book is dedicated to my wife, Donna, who prior to and early in our marriage accepted my narrow and fundamentalist beliefs and was baptized into my church and way of life. What a joy it has been to have her struggle with me, confront our doubts, and together seek a different path.

This book is dedicated to my two adult children, Tim and Debbie, who were raised in our evangelical/fundamentalist Christian home, went to churches with those teachings, and attended ORU while I was a faculty member there. I am so impressed with them that as adults they are also able to evaluate critically their upbringing and modify their beliefs to something with which they can be comfortable. It is also dedicated to their spouses who are together joining this wonderful yet challenging theological expedition.

This book is dedicated to individuals who are or have been deeply engaged in evangelical/fundamentalist Christianity and struggle with their faith but feel they cannot change or escape. I understand. I've been there. It was not until around age 45 that I finally gained the strength to begin challenging my deeply held beliefs. My theological evolution has been slow and often uncomfortable. It has been a 25-year struggle from my former belief system to a more progressive Christianity. During this time I have often vacillated between wondering if I had better stop my questioning and return to my evangelical/fundamentalist Christian roots or should I totally abandon my Christian faith and become an agnostic. This book is dedicated to those who might gain courage from my journey to begin or continue one of their own. Ultimately, this book is dedicated to those who want to more genuinely follow the way of the life and teachings of Jesus and put aside the doctrines and beliefs that divide, discriminate, and alienate.

TABLE OF CONTENTS

At the trial of Jesus, Pilate asks the classic question, "What is truth?"

(John 18:38)

THE BEGINNING OF A JOURNEY

"I've been lied to by my church and I am mad about it," was the opening of a conversation I had with a friend my wife and I had not seen for 30 years. In the late 1960's we had attended the same evangelical/fundamentalist church, and after we moved to another state, had only kept in contact at Christmas. "I believed the church's interpretation of the Bible," she said. "I believed in a personal God and thought that if I honored God in my life; confessed Jesus as Lord and Savior; believed in the scriptures relative to healing, prosperity, and God's personal protection and care for me; and prayed regularly, my life would be all right. And now, here I am, 65 years old, my first husband divorced me for another woman and left me with three children. After my children were raised, I remarried only to have my second husband die. My son has been in and out of prison, and I won't trouble you with the rest of my issues. And I'm supposed to still believe in the promises in the Bible? My church has lied to me...they have not told me the truth!"

This conversation came at a time in my life when I, too, was examining my doubts, concerns, and questions about the Bible and the theology I had been taught. I was contemplating Socrates' classic statement made over 300 years before the birth of Jesus, "An unexamined life is not worth living." I was bothered by the same questions our friend was asking. For Socrates, people who do not examine truth and question and reflect on their basic beliefs and values, live a superficial life. They are wasting the precious life they have been given; and therefore, such a life is not worth living. What is interesting is that Socrates is reported to have made these comments at his trial, which ultimately condemned him to death. He was accused and found guilty of not believing in the gods of his culture and state, and corrupting the minds of the youth of Athens. Rather than recant or apologize, he is reported to have made this classic statement and then accepted his death sentence. It is interesting that some 400 years later at the trial of Jesus, when Jesus says he specifically came to speak truth, Pilate asks the classic question, "What is truth?" (John 18:38) Today, many are asking the same question, especially as it relates to the Bible and theology.

I recall an important event in the first month of graduate school in 1965. In response to a question from the professor in a class discussion, I said, "most people know that ..." He immediately interrupted and asked me, "How do you know that most people know that? What is the evidence?" It was that challenge to my statement that I never forgot. It made a significant impact on me. How do you know? What is true? What is the evidence?

For most of my life, I have ostensibly lived in two worlds of truth. First, I was born and raised and lived in an environment of a very powerful belief system that clearly stated that what the Bible says is true, totally, completely, and without question. We believed, as is stated by the Assembly of God, that: "The Bible is the Word of God written; it is the revelation of the truths of God conveyed by inspiration through his servants to us. As such, it is *infallible* and without error.... We conceive the Bible to be in actuality the very Word of God.... We define inerrancy as meaning "exempt from error" and infallibility as "incapable of error".... Such inerrancy and infallibility apply to all of scripture.... It is truth." (Accessed from the Internet October 10, 2011)

The Community Bible Church in Montevideo, MN, that my father began in 1956 when I was in the eighth grade, has a simpler, but similar belief statement about the Bible: "The Bible is the only inspired, infallible, and authoritative Word of God." (Accessed from the Internet February 28, 2012)

It is important to note that this belief about the Bible is not unique to the Assembly of God or the Community Bible Church in which I was primarily raised. The Evangelical Free Church of America states that "God has spoken in the scriptures, both Old and New Testaments, through the words of human authors. As the verbally inspired Word of God, the Bible is without error...the ultimate...to be believed in all that it teaches, obeyed in all that it requires, and trusted in all that it promises." (Accessed from the Internet July 25, 2012) The evangelical Wheaton College states that the "scriptures of the Old and New Testaments are verbally inspired by God and inerrant...are fully trustworthy and of supreme and final authority in all they say." (Accessed from the Internet July 25, 2012)

I was taught, as are most evangelical and fundamentalist Christians, to believe that whatever the Bible says is true. It was true when the Bible was written 2000 plus years ago and is still true today. Its truth never changes. Anything that contradicts the Bible cannot be true. The Bible is true regardless of any evidence that would question its truthfulness and is also true even if there is lack of evidence to verify its truthfulness. If the Bible records that God took a rib from Adam and created Eve (Genesis 2:21-22), this happened exactly as it is stated. If the Bible says that Noah built a big boat and saved two of all the animals on earth from a flood that covered the entire earth (Genesis 6-8), then this happened exactly as it is recorded. If the sun stood still for a full day so Israel could win a battle (Joshua 10:13), it surely happened. And if an analysis of the Bible concludes that the Earth and Universe were formed about 6000 years ago, then that is true regardless of any findings of science.

As a child and initially as an adult, I accepted this belief without question. After all, I thought, where else could you find how to live your life and how to get to heaven if not in the Bible. God told us in the Bible that he "...so loved the world that he gave his one and only Son that whosoever believes in him shall not perish but have eternal life." (John 3:16) And, the Bible reports that Jesus himself said, "I am the way and the truth and the life. No one comes to the Father except through me." (John 14:6) It sure sounded good to me! A pretty simple belief statement required for admission to heaven someday. With affection for the Bible, I read, memorized, and studied it and attempted to follow its precepts.

I recognize that for many Christians, the idea of the literal interpretation of the Bible is incomprehensible since for them the Bible has never been the absolute, written Word of God. If you understand the Bible from this viewpoint, you probably won't be able to fully identify with the perspective from which I am writing.

For my family and me, the concept of the Bible as ultimate truth was drilled deeply into our minds and sub-consciousnesses at home and in church. The motto of "Jesus is the answer" rang true to us regardless of the question. Growing up, I had little problem with this idea and fully accepted the Bible as the absolute Word of God. If we wanted to know the truth, we would search for it in the Bible. To question anything in the Bible was paramount to denying the authority of God Almighty. To question the Bible was surely the first step in "going to hell." Looking back, my Christian faith was something I "inherited." To be completely honest, I did not choose it. It was given me on a daily basis and I accepted it as "the way, the truth, and the life." (John 14:6) As stated by Richo, (2011) the unfortunate evidence is that the faith most adults follow is the one they were given as children. To develop an "adult faith" is "an onerous task...and there are few trusted soul-mates to befriend during this lonely and bewildering journey" of growing up. (O'Murchu, p. 3)

On the other hand, while my child and young adulthood were

deeply grounded in very conservative, evangelical Christianity, my college education, including earning a bachelor's degree, two master's degrees, and a doctorate, taught me the concept that truth is based upon evidence, and needs to be verified. Before you determine whether something is true, you objectively gather evidence and you apply probability statistics to the evidence. If you have a level of confidence of at least 95% that something is true, only then can you accept it as truth. You don't accept truth by faith. Even then, if a research study shows that a finding is at the 95% level of confidence, you are still not done. You merely accept it as true for the moment and will always be open to new studies, new ideas, new concepts that might indicate a different truth. This method of thinking often makes the person not trained in the academic method of determining truth distressed or confused since truth appears always to be changing. One research study will show that some substance is healthy for you only to have another study years later show that it is not. It is not that truth changes, but our understanding of truth often changes. In ancient times it was firmly believed that the earth was the center of the universe. It was a truth that was completely accepted until it was discovered that this concept was actually false. How difficult it was to accept this new-found truth; especially since entire theological belief systems had been built around the old earth-centric concept. Individuals who accepted the new truth were condemned, imprisoned, and faced the possibility of death.

One can understand why those who ascribe to fundamentalism in their faith journey are often opposed to public education and especially higher education. They fear too much critical thinking might lead people away from their faith. My parents and others of my childhood faith often spoke against the "sins of education," and how too much education caused individuals to leave the faith. How interesting it was to hear a 2012 presidential candidate state such a position. In an hour-long interview with conservative television host Glenn Beck, Rick Santorum said, "I understand why Barack Obama wants to send every kid to college, because of their indoctrination mills…. The indoctrination that is going on at the university level is harmful to our country." (Kaplan) Since the focus of fundamentalism is to tell individuals what to think and believe, they seem to be threatened by higher education with its emphasis of encouraging individuals to think for themselves.

And so it was; on the one hand, I had accepted truth being what the Bible says regardless of how "extreme" it sounded; and on the other hand, I was trained to accept truth that was well documented, based on an abundance of evidence gathered from objective research, having a good level of confidence after applying probability statistics. These two competing methods of discovering "truths" often led to internal conflict. For the first 40 to 50 years of my life, I was reasonably successful in accepting this contradiction. But, there came a point in middle age when I could no longer believe without questioning the truths that I had accepted from the church, which was interpreting Biblical truths and communicating them to its followers. The Bible suggests that "whatever is true, whatever is noble, whatever is right, whatever is pure…think about such things." (Philippians 4:8) But what is truth? What is noble? And what is right and pure?

I needed to begin an in-depth inquiry about truth and examine my basic beliefs and values. Are they indeed my own or are they what I've blindly accepted from my parents, conservative churches, and others? Was the indoctrination of my belief system from my childhood so deep that I would not be able to penetrate or challenge those beliefs? Could I objectively examine my deepest held beliefs? Is, as Socrates said, living an unexamined life with an unexamined belief system wasting the precious life that we've each been given?

I am reminded of my childhood food likes and dislikes. I would not eat any kind of salad dressing, onions, mustard, or pickles, to name just a few items. Why? Because my parents did not eat these, did not like them, so I did not like them either; or at least so I thought. As an adult, I was surprised that as I tried each of these items, I discovered I actually did like them. How much of what we believe as adults comes to us unexamined from our childhood? To what extent do we live our entire lives never examining the soundness of what we learned as children? For me I was in my 40's before I felt the need to examine my beliefs. Had I indiscriminately accepted as truth what I learned as a child? Had I really thought through my beliefs?

In this process I began to read books and journals written by scholars, philosophers, and theologians who in many cases have spent their entire lifetime studying theology and philosophy. These subjects have been the focus of examination since time began; they are not new. These writers speak to these issues with much greater insight and understanding than I with my limited background and education in these areas. But, I needed not only to read about the interpretations others have given to these issues, I needed to discuss and write out my own thoughts and ideas. One of the great joys I've had over the past 20 years is that as I've read and contemplated these issues, I've discovered many others whose life experiences challenge what they've learned in church. We've had many wonderful and sometimes apprehensive discussions as we've read many books and explored ideas that challenged our beliefs. It was liberating to me to realize that others had similar doubts and questions, but they too, were hesitant (or reluctant or afraid) to voice their concerns often for fear of being labeled a heretic or being ostracized by family and friends.

Changing one's deeply held beliefs is not an easy journey. It is not easy to leave one's comfort zone. It is painful to "let go" of one's core dogmas. It is much easier to not even consider a change. Parker Palmer (2008) suggests that when one becomes disillusioned by experience that leads one to reconsider one's beliefs, the journey takes one away from fiction and fantasy toward reality and truth. He indicates, however, that these experiences can be very painful. Especially helpful during this process has been in-depth conversations with close friends and my wife and two adult children. They have questioned some of my opinions, which gave me pause to re-think some thoughts. We have had great conversations.

While these conversations have challenged and assisted me in my spiritual journey and provided clarity, I understand that others will reach different conclusions. I do recognize, as noted by Tickle (2008), with the emergence of the progressive Christianity movement, there is also a backlash violently pushing back. I have experienced rejection by some of my former fundamentalist friends. Resistance to change and new ideas has always accompanied any transformation. My thoughts and reflections represent the understanding I have today of truth; especially as it relates to the Bible. Since understanding changes based on new insights, these thoughts are not set in concrete.

The first challenge in this journey is my upbringing; my years entrenched in evangelical Christianity and its deep psychological impact. Whenever anyone would question a Biblical interpretation (in reality the church's or pastor's interpretation) of truth, the person was quickly chastised and scriptures quoted such as, "the fool says in his heart there is no God," (Psalms 14:1) or "God gave them over to a depraved mind." (Romans 1:28) The Bible is full of passages that condemn anyone who challenges its authority. Bawer (1997) makes a key observation that I can confirm accurate from my experience. He says, "Fundamentalist, evangelical, and charismatic Christianity demands believers, not thinkers…no evidence, no logic, no personal experience, nothing can change their mind about 'revealed truth.' Questioning 'revealed truth' in any way challenges the belief system at its core. The more successfully any 'revealed truth' is challenged, the more vehemently the challenge must be rejected." (p. 8-9)

Evaluating ones religious beliefs also means you are inadvertently making statements about the beliefs of others. This is especially painful when it is the deeply held beliefs of your parents and siblings. How do you disagree with beliefs that have been the focus of their entire life? My loving siblings have ever so kindly told me, "we are very concerned for you," and "we are very saddened about your disillusionment with the teachings you were taught growing up." I am concerned and saddened as well. But I can no longer remain silent on such an important issue as "is the Bible the Word of God, to be read literally, and accepted without question?" Perhaps it was the book written by Meyers, (*Saving Jesus from the Church*) that finally convinced me that I must speak up. Meyers writes a very challenging book discussing how the conservative/evangelical church of today has so distorted the teachings of Jesus, that we don't recognize Jesus. He also stresses that these churches have gained so much power, especially with their domination on TV and radio, that moderate Christians must speak up against these radical beliefs. And so I am. As Borg puts it, "what is at stake…is the future of Christianity as well as the future of our country." (*Speaking Christian*, p. 236)

Carlton Pearson, a student I knew and a graduate of Oral Roberts University (ORU) who founded and was the pastor of a large evangelical/charismatic church in Tulsa for 20 years before leaving it for a more progressive view of the Bible and theology, wrote in his book, "What is needed is a 'stepping back' and a brutal re-examination of the so-called truths of Christianity, the religion of my birth that I have loved all my life, and [seeing that] it has some deep, staggering dysfunctions." (2010, p. 26) Central to this re-examination for me was the question, "Is the Bible the written Word of God?"

Steve Jobs told a graduating class at Stanford University, "Your time is limited, so don't waste it living someone else's life. Don't be trapped by dogma—which is living the results of other people's thinking. Don't let the noise of others drown out your own inner voice. And most important, have the courage to follow your heart and intuition."

This is a personal story of my Christian journey. I felt "trapped by dogma" and it was time to evaluate whether or not I was living someone else's belief system. As deeply as I believed in, read, studied, and memorized the Bible, I often wondered; is the Bible really the actual Word of God? I describe what I was taught as a child; having spent the first 50 years of my life in very conservative Christianity, including being raised in a Pentecostal pastor's home, being a church youth group leader, an elder in a church, singing in a gospel quartet, giving sermons in church, and being on the faculty at Oral Roberts University (ORU) for 14 years from age 31 to 45. This story began as a journal in 1993 when at the age of 50 I decided it was time to honestly look at the doubts and concerns I had been ignoring for years about my Christian beliefs and particularly the question, "Is the Bible the literal, inerrant, written, Word of God?" For years I had swept under the rug all questions about the many strange and conflicting statements and stories in the Bible. Did God actually say those words found in the Bible? Can we completely and totally trust what the Bible says? Is it relevant today? What is truth? It was time to reconsider and re-evaluate the Bible.

Ralph Peters (p. xi) says, "I do not write to impress my thoughts on others, but to challenge myself to discover what I truly think. The act of writing forces us to think more deeply and more clearly than we otherwise would do, and to provoke independent thought in readers. I learn by writing." These are my thoughts. They make sense to me. I hope the sharing of my personal transformation, the evidence, including real-world experience, of why I had to let go of the Bible as the literal, inerrant, written Word of God, and my being reborn into an adult, progressive Christian faith, may cause the reader to carefully and critically evaluate their own belief system.

Note: *In this book I will often use the terms charismatic/evangelical/fundamental/conservative as somewhat the same. I do understand that as they describe Christianity, they are not the same and are not monolithic. I realize that various beliefs are held within these terms, however, for this book, they describe a rather common view of the Bible. In general they see the Bible as the literal, written, Word of God and practice what Smith calls "Biblicism." (2011)*

Is the Bible the Word of God?

When I was a child, I talked like a child, I thought like a child, I reasoned like a child. When I became a man, I put childish ways behind me.

(I Corinthians 13:11)

Chapter One
PUT CHILDISH WAYS BEHIND

I often think about what we were taught and what we learned as children and to what extent are we able to "put childish ways behind." Consider some of the classic stories that are read to children. Everyone knows the story of Snow White. She is born to a queen who soon after her birth dies. The king remarries and his new wife (Snow White's stepmother) is jealous of the beauty of Snow White and after several attempts to kill her, she is successful in causing her to fall into a deep sleep. Snow White is finally saved by a handsome prince. They get married and live happily ever after.

We see the same theme repeated in the Cinderella story. Her mother dies, her father remarries a woman with two daughters, and then he dies. Cinderella becomes the "slave" of the stepmother and stepsisters until she is rescued by another handsome prince and they get married and live happily ever after. Does the message of these stories affect our children? When our granddaughter was 4 years old, she told her mother, "I want to get married in a white dress to a prince and live happily ever after!" These stories do make an impact.

Hansel and Gretel are the young children of a poor woodcutter. Their mother had died and their father had remarried. Again, it's a stepmother who seeks to get rid of the children by dropping them off in the woods and not returning to pick them up. The children wander into a gingerbread house belonging to a wicked witch who plans to eat them. They kill the witch, escape, take the wealth of the witch with them, return home to find their stepmother dead, and live happily ever after with their father.

Innocent stories indoctrinate our children early in life. If one is a child, you had better hope your mother never dies, and if she does, you better do everything you can to keep your father from marrying again. For if he does, you are in trouble. Stepmothers are portrayed very negatively. They are going to try to kill you! But, thank heavens for Prince Charming who, according to these stories, can save the girls from their plight.

I think about the story and the role of Santa Claus in the lives of children. He is watching you all the time and if you are good, he will come at Christmas and bring you gifts. Then there is the Easter Bunny. What a wonderful bunny this is who brings such delightful sweets at Easter. Of course, we can't forget the Tooth Fairy. If you are a good child and lose teeth, you can put them under your pillow and magically in the morning when you awake there will be money under your pillow.

At some point, we realize these are just stories and are not really true. It is the parents who give presents at Christmas, chocolate Easter bunnies at Easter, and put money under the pillow. But I wonder if there are lasting negative affects upon relationships with stepmothers? Or what about what parents teach us about race? I am reminded of the deeply insightful words found in a song in the wonderful musical, "South Pacific."

You've got to be taught
To hate and fear,
You've got to be taught
From year to year,
It's got to be drummed
In your dear little ear
You've got to be carefully taught.

You've got to be taught to be afraid
Of people whose eyes are oddly made,
And people whose skin is a different shade,
You've got to be carefully taught.

You've got to be taught before it's too late,
Before you are six or seven or eight,
To hate all the people your relatives hate,
You've got to be carefully taught!

I often reflect on that phase, "You've got to be carefully taught." I think about religious stories that we learn at home and in our churches. "When I was a child, I talked like a child, I thought like a child, I reasoned like a child. When I became a man, I put childish ways behind me." I wonder what "childish ways" are we to put behind us? Which ones are we to keep?

In evangelical churches, we are taught that the Bible is the Word of God, without error, and to be taken literally. As a child that works pretty well. In 6 days God created the heavens and earth, man and woman, trees and animals. We learn stories of how God destroyed all living things in a flood but saved Noah, his family, and a pair of every living thing in a special ark; how Abraham was planning to sacrifice his son Isaac until God intervened; how God led Israel from Egypt to the promised land killing tens of thousands of men, women, and children along the way; how Daniel was saved in the lion's den; the virgin birth of Jesus; the miracles he performed, as well as his death and resurrection. We learn about the rapture and the battle of Armageddon. If we believe and are baptized, we will go to heaven when we die while most of the rest of humankind will burn in hell. In the rapture, we will go to heaven and they will be "left behind." As evangelicals, we learn that our way is the only way. Are any of these stories and beliefs to be "put behind us"?

Why is it that so often individuals mature physically and mentally, but seem to never mature theologically? They live an adult life with an elementary school Christian education. Fundamentalist Christian churches often use faith as a device for manipulation rather than for maturation. Too much education is frowned upon. Public education is criticized as "liberal" and many children are sent to Christian schools or home schooled for continued indoctrination. When we become adults, many continue to believe these Bible stories we learned as children to be factual. Some accept all the stories, some accept many of the stories but "put away" others, and a few reject these stories totally just as they no longer believe in Santa Claus or the Tooth Fairy. The process of making these adult decisions relative to the Bible is often a soul-searching endeavor. It certainly has been for me. The first churches I attended as an adult continued to promote the literal, factual interpretation of the Bible and gave me no encouragement to "think for myself." For most of the first 45 years of my life, I resisted any urges to give birth to my doubts, to grow up theologically. Now I reflect almost daily, "what childish ways do I need to put behind me"?

My mother died at age 89 in May of 2009. My two older brothers, two younger sisters, and I wrote about Mom for her memorial. She "had a simple, incredible faith" we wrote. She taught us "don't question, analyze, or try to figure it out; just believe and trust in the Lord." Since her "born again" experience as a teenager, she totally accepted the Bible as the Word of God, without error, and to be taken literally. While I am happy for my mother and for those who have a "simple faith," for better or worse, for me, my faith is not simple. However, I feel I am in good company; Saint Augustine in his 4th century "Confessions" wrote that he never found total certainty in his faith, nor did Mother Theresa in the 20th century.

But what does it really mean to have a "simple faith?" Is it a positive attribute? I suppose not thinking or allowing one's mind to consider any of our doubts is mentally effortless. Accepting what one has been taught is easy and comforting. Unfortunately, when taken to the extreme, individuals with a "simple faith" have often been gullible to heresy and followed leaders with strange and sometimes dangerous theologies. People with "simple faith" followed David Koresh to their deaths in Waco, TX; 913 followers of Jim Jones committed mass suicide in Jonestown, Guyana in 1978; followers of Warren Jeffs, president of the Fundamentalist Church of Jesus Christ of the Latter Day Saints, promoted men having sexual activity with multiple minors. Followers of a "simple faith" have supported slavery, become suicide bombers, flown planes into the World Trade Center buildings, and shot doctors who performed abortions. Individuals have refused medical care and died since they believe in the literal interpretation of the Bible and expect God to heal them. Others have believed God would provide for all their needs and did not plan for retirement only to run out of money and need the family or government to take care of them. How many have sold all their possessions believing that the rapture was happening on a specific date or giving their life savings to a televangelist expecting a miracle? There are pit falls to a "simple faith."

It is my nature to reflect on and explore ideas, something I have enjoyed during my 40 years of employment at universities where the focus is on the "exploration of ideas." For, if an idea, a belief, or an action cannot survive the scrutiny of examination, perhaps it is not something worth keeping. I remember my brother-in-law once said to me, "Brynteson, you think too much!" I accept that observation which occasionally results in sleepless nights! But relative to theology, as was the case for O'Murchu, "I began to think for myself, read more extensively, and explore questions of religious meaning, which…earlier I had not dared to do…the childlike beliefs no longer nourished, inspired, or challenged me." (2010, p.3)

While I "repressed" my concerns and questions relative to theology for many years, beginning in my early 40's and continuing over the past 25 years, I've begun to evaluate my faith and allow myself to explore my doubts and concerns. If you have never had any doubts, perhaps you can't relate to my thoughts or journey. Maybe I'm a "heretic" destined for eternal torment. Maybe I'll be "left behind." However, if you've ever had any questions about your faith, perhaps my observations might "give you permission" to allow yourself to also examine your faith more critically. Of the many who have influenced my spiritual search, Phillip Yancy writes, "I have spent most of my life in recovery from the church." (2001, p.1) He writes how his brother did not recover from a Christian fundamentalist childhood and as an adult became an agnostic. Anne Lamott puts it this way, "When I was a child, I thought grown-ups and teachers knew the truth…It took years for me to discover that the first step in finding out the truth is to begin unlearning almost everything adults had taught me." (p. 1) So, I reflect, "What childish ways should and am I able to put behind me and yet remain a 'Christian?'" And, can the sharing of my theological evolution encourage others to also evaluate what childish ways they might leave behind?

You've got to be taught...
From year to year,
Its got to be drummed
In your dear little ear...
You've got to be taught before it's too
late,
Before you are six or seven or eight...
You've got to be carefully taught!

—Lyrics from "You've Got To Be Carefully Taught"
in *South Pacific*

Chapter Two

YOU'VE GOT TO BE CAREFULLY TAUGHT

Growing up in a very conservative, fundamentalist, evangelical Christian home and church, the most important book in our home was the Bible, the "Word of God." We read it every day and memorized portions of it. The answer to almost all, if not all questions could be found in the Bible. The center of our life was the Bible and our church. It governed our lives. We attended church Sunday morning, Sunday night, and Wednesday night. Being born again was critical so we would not be "left behind" in the soon-to-come rapture. Every attempt was made to separate ourselves from the world and its influence. Growing up, there never was another child or young person from my school who attended our church, so all my friends came from outside the church. I was instructed to be very careful to not become too friendly with them.

While a high school education was important, higher education was suspect since it would lead one away from the Bible as one's only source for truth, unless higher education was a Bible school, which was acceptable. We were taught that many behaviors were sins and were to be avoided. Some of these sins or moral issues could be found in the Bible, but many were not.

It was a sin to go to a movie. I was 17 years old before I went to my first movie. I was with my high school senior class on a graduation trip from Minnesota to Chicago. Away from home, I decided it was time to experience this sin—a movie. With some trepidation, I went to my first movie, *Ben Hur*. It was in a theater with a velvet curtain, chandeliers hanging from the ceiling, and wonderful cushioned seats. I remember thinking, why is this a sin? What's so bad about going to this movie? Is this what it's like to sin? Perhaps movies are not so bad! I decided maybe going to a movie was not a sin. I wondered if what I was being taught at home was really correct. However, it is important to mention that the teaching of movies being sinful was so deep that it was 6 years before I went to a movie again. You've got to be carefully taught!

Growing up, we were taught that for a woman to wear any make-up or jewelry was a sin, another moral issue. Some other churches allowed the wearing of make-up, but these women were all going to hell. Our women dressed plainly and were going to heaven. I remember vividly a sermon I heard when I was probably 10 years old. "Dog meat!!" That's what the preacher said would happen to women who wore make-up as he used scriptures of the story of Jezebel from the Old Testament (II Kings 9) to back up his claim. It was not until I was in my 20's that I decided that perhaps wearing make-up was not a sin. Another moral issue bit the dust.

Going to a bowling alley and bowling was a sin. Then, about the time I was a sophomore in high school, my hometown of Montevideo built a new bowling facility. I didn't tell my parents, but I began bowling with 3 other friends every Saturday morning in a high school league. Eventually my parents found out and somehow, bless their hearts, I was able to convince them that it was all right, and bowling was no longer a sin. WOW! That was an easy change in moral values and another moral issue off the list.

I grew up playing Rook; a card game that was acceptable for Christians with beliefs like ours since playing with "real" cards was a sin, another moral issue. In high school I began to play spades, hearts, and whist with "real" cards. I had to keep it a secret from my parents since if they knew, I no longer would have been able to associate with my friends. I never could see the moral problem with playing cards, whether with Rook cards or "real" cards. I just thought I must be a morally bad person since I didn't see the problem, but to stay out of trouble with my parents, I kept that to myself. I sometimes wondered if I would be "left behind." You've got to be carefully taught!

What a sinner I was becoming since I no longer saw movies, make-up, bowling, or "real" cards as sins. Dancing was a sin, so I never went to a dance growing up. Listening to secular music was certainly suspect. In our home, we only listened to Christian music. For some attending our church, "mixed" swimming was a sin. Fortunately, my parents didn't follow that one. Smoking and alcohol consumption were sins. The issue was not that they were bad for one's health. No, they were a sin! I was 45 years old before I had my first beer and first glass of wine. And, of course, sex outside of marriage (fornication), homosexuality, divorce, and abortion, were especially grievous sins. Thank God that playing sports was not a sin. It was the love of my life and was what kept me sane as a child. My senior year in high school I was fortunate to be named to the all-conference teams in football, basketball, and baseball and earn a football scholarship to college.

My point in discussing the issue of sins is that I had questions about the teachings relative to the Christian beliefs I was receiving as a child and teenager. The seeds of doubt about what my church and parents were teaching me were planted as a child and would grow within me over many years, but I would not act on any of these doubts until I was over 40 years of age. "You've got to be carefully taught," or as Proverbs puts it, "train a child in the way he should go, and when he is old he will not turn from it." (Proverbs 22:6) Even though "When I became a man, I put childish ways behind me," that has been a soul-searching process. O'Muruchu makes an interesting observation that often it is retirement before people "feel safe enough to…take a risk that might involve changes in life direction that just felt too scary at an earlier time." (p. 10-11) What do I keep? What do I leave behind? Will I be left behind?

Looking back, while I had many doubts and concerns, I have the greatest respect and love for my parents as well as my brothers and sisters. My parents did what they believed to be "right" and did so with a great deal of love. I have no regrets or disappointment over my fundamentalist upbringing. One time as a child when I was especially taxing on my mother, she grabbed me, hugged me, and with tears said, "Can't you be a nice boy for mommy? You know I love you and Jesus loves you!" She did not yell, punish, express anger, or threaten me with the fires of hell. Rather, she demonstrated her unconditional love and showed me that nothing I could do could take that away. She showed me how Christ feels when we are problem children. He cries, hugs us, and pleads with us to do better. That experience overcame the legalism in which I was raised and I'm sure kept me from being a rebellious child. Mom indeed, had a "simple faith" and never questioned anything about her faith and what she had been taught. While Dad would occasionally allow himself to "question," he would soon stop and say with deep conviction and a hint of anger, "No, we can't go there. Don't get involved in controversies we don't understand." I believe he was afraid of where that questioning might take him. But as much as I respected my parents and as deep as the love was that I felt from my parents, I wrestled with the basic belief system and especially our authority, the Bible, the inerrant Word of God.

There came a point in my life that I could no longer accept "no we can't go there." I had seen too much pain and violence caused by following the Bible as the inerrant Word of God; too many problems to overlook. I could not have that kind of simple, blind faith, unwilling to put my belief system to the test. Perhaps I saw in my dad a fear to question his beliefs. In his 80's he expressed some bitterness over his decision to go into the ministry. He occasionally indicated he should have kept the good job he had out of high school and should have not left it to preach. Perhaps his cautiously expressed regrets contributed to the motivation for me to examine my beliefs and to reflect on what I could leave behind. I did not want to have regrets. Central to that process, I needed to especially explore the question of whether the Bible is the literal, inerrant Word of God. Is it the authority for our life?

Our planet has just over 6 billion persons. Of 22 major religions, there are approximately:
- 2.2 billion Christians (32%)
- 1.6 billion Muslims (23%)
- 1.1 billion Agnostics, atheists, or nonreligious (16%)
- 1 billion Hindu's (15%)
- 500 million Buddhists (7%)
- 400 million Chinese traditional religion (6%)
- 14 million Jews (.2%)

According to the Pew Forum on Religion and Public Life, (Accessed June 30, 2012), there are approximately 41,000 Christian denominations worldwide. Just think, 41,000 different Christian churches believe they have the truth! Of the 22 major world religions, the vast majority of the believers are the same religion of the family into which they were born and/or raised. Clearly, very few people give serious thought to whether or not their religion, their belief is the "correct" one. They believe what they have been taught from childhood is "correct" without ever putting their faith to the test. How sad.

This is how it will be at the coming of the Son of Man. Two men will be in the field; one will be taken and the other left behind.

(Matthew 24: 39-40)

Chapter Three

LEFT BEHIND IN THE RAPTURE

The idea of the rapture, when Jesus takes his believers from earth to heaven, and the possibility of being left behind was drilled into my consciousness from an early age. Even though I was only five years old in 1948, I can remember my family sitting in the living room in our small pastor's parsonage in Minden, Nebraska listening to the radio as Israel became a nation. I recall the exuberance of my parents over this announcement and the joy they expressed since according to their interpretation of the Bible relative to this event, the rapture would be soon and the end of the world was imminent. I didn't fully realize what all this meant, other than we were soon to go to heaven, I would not live on this earth much longer, and hopefully I'd not be left behind. I remember thinking about how I'd miss swimming at the pool, running in the Nebraska wheat fields in the summer, and playing with our dog Teddy. Yet, I also thought about "am I really good enough to go to heaven"? Although I didn't really dwell on it much, it was always in the back of my mind.

When our family moved to Manitowoc, Wisconsin in 1950 where my dad accepted the pastorate of a church, I remember the constant background "noise" of the rapture. It was preached and talked about in conversations, and this looming event was a constant theme in our home and church. Even so, it did not detract from our family having fun, such as playing at the beach on Lake Michigan and enjoying the wonderful softball games, ice skating, ping pong, and numerous sports in which we participated. Yet I wondered, would I be left behind?

In 1956 when we moved to Montevideo, Minnesota where my

dad began a new church, the theme of the rapture and Armageddon was a continuing part of our life and thoughts. Members of the congregation would routinely prophesy that Jesus was coming soon, we needed to forsake our evil ways, and we needed to get ready. Some would speak in tongues and another would interpret warning us of the coming Armageddon and rapture. The theme was this is imminent and we must get ready or we might get left behind. As a teenager, these warnings and messages began to have their effect on me, and I began to believe that certainly within the next few years Jesus would return. I needed to make sure my confessions were complete and up-to-date and my belief in Jesus Christ as my Lord and Savior was strong with no doubts. So, while I prepared for the rapture, I also engaged in high school sports with gusto since more than likely with our going to heaven, the sports would be over and the joy of being with Jesus would be so fantastic that I would soon not miss my love of sports. At least I hoped this would be true. I did love sports and rather hated to have to give them up. I really was not interested in a mansion in heaven or walking on streets of gold, but I also did not want to burn in hell.

As I went to college in 1961, married Donna, my high school sweetheart, then attended graduate school in 1965, and had two children, in the back of my mind was the persistent thought that any day Christ would return and all that schooling would be wasted. I often wondered what is the point of having children and going to graduate school to plan for a teaching career. In 1967 when Israel captured Jerusalem in the six-day war, the end-time messages from the pulpits and books were everywhere in evangelical circles. Our pastor of the Assemblies of God church that we attended in Springfield, Massachusetts spoke with convincing clarity using current events and scriptures that Jesus would return to rapture Christians to heaven in no later than seven years with Jerusalem coming under

Jewish control. Therefore, his return would be no later than 1974. His prophetic words were echoed by many other evangelicals. It had a great impact on Donna and me.

In 1968 when I had everything completed for my doctoral degree except the finishing of my dissertation, I chose to look for a teaching position and complete my degree while teaching. (I did finish it and was awarded the doctorate in 1969.) While I had several job opportunities in New England and on the East Coast, feeling that the end of the world was near, I accepted a job at South Dakota State University to be near family. As I mentioned, believing that the "end" was near influenced my life, my thinking, and my decisions. I continued my association with evangelical churches in Brookings since they had beliefs about the rapture, the literal interpretation of the Bible, and a fairly strict moral code. I felt I had to attend the "correct" churches and believe the right things so I would not be left behind.

In 1970, in an attempt to become as familiar as possible with end time theology, I began studying Revelation and other books in the Bible and carefully read *The Late Great Planet Earth*, by Hal Lindsey published in 1970. He interpreted the Bible in light of current events and while not specifically giving a time table for the rapture, the specifics of the antichrist, and the battle of Armageddon, he made it very clear that all these events would be within months and probably no longer than a few years, and for sure, no longer than one generation of the founding of the state of Israel in 1948. For certain, from his analysis, the rapture would occur by 1988. Considering that the second coming of Christ had been an essential part of my upbringing since I was five years old, it seemed to all make sense to me. I did not want to be left behind; yet, in all honesty I was not overwhelmingly excited about the rapture since I felt I was young and had a life to live and a family to raise.

With the end times ever present in my mind, even though I did not actively discuss these thoughts and emotions, I accepted a teaching position at Oral Roberts University (ORU) in 1974. What better place to be than the Mecca of Evangelical Christianity to complete my final days on earth; being isolated from the "world" in our Christian enclave where the Bible's promises of healing from all diseases and prosperity were abundant. As 1974 progressed to 1975 and then into the 1980's and with all these prophetic events not taking place, seeds of doubt began to arise. These doubts, coupled with my observations that the promises of healing at ORU never happened for individuals with organic diseases such as cerebral palsy, muscular dystrophy, and individuals who were paraplegic and quadriplegic, I began to wonder, maybe all these prophecies are misinterpretations of the Bible, and all these promises about health and healing don't really work. Maybe the Bible should not be taken literally.

As a person trained in the scientific method of verifying truth, I began to apply reason and experience to scripture. This was blasphemy in my family and in evangelical Christianity. With great fear for my own soul, I allowed my mind to quietly and privately question the scriptures wondering all the time if, as a consequence I would be left behind if the rapture came.

It is important to understand the powerful psychological impact of the "left behind" narrative. The thought of being "left behind" can lead one to suppress any doubts or concerns about the Bible as being the Word of God. One dare not question the Bible. In recent years, discussions with my two adult children indicate that growing up, the rapture was also on their minds. They speak of sometimes coming home to an empty house and worrying that perhaps the rapture had occurred and they'd been left behind.

I have since become aware that end times prophecies have been around for a very long time. The disciples expected Jesus to return during their lifetime. In the 1500's Martin Luther indicated that while he didn't know the precise day of the end, he was certain that the time was very near. George Rapp predicted that Jesus would begin his reign on earth in 1829. William Miller said the second coming of Christ was to be in 1844; Charles Russell said it would be in 1874; Herbert W. Armstrong predicted it to be in 1975; and Nostradamus said it would be 1999.

As previously noted, Hal Lindsey had predicted the rapture by 1988. In 1978 Chuck Smith, Pastor of Calvary Chapel in Costa Mesa, California, predicted the rapture in 1981. In the 1970's Pat Robertson predicted that the world would end in the fall of 1982. Lester Sumrall, in his 1987 book *I Predict 2000 AD*, predicted that Jerusalem would be the richest city on Earth, that the Common Market would rule Europe, and that there would be a nuclear war involving Russia and perhaps the US. He also prophesied that the greatest Christian revival in the history of the church would happen, all during the last 13 years of the 20th century. Edgar Whisenaut, a NASA scientist, published the book *88 Reasons Why the Rapture Will Be in 1988*. It sold over 4 million copies and probably made him a multimillionaire. In 1999 Jerry Falwell said the rapture would be by 2009; Harold Camping said it would be in 1994, and when that didn't happen he revised it to 2011, specifically, May 21. Jack Van Impe has indicated a number of times that Jesus would return within a certain period of time but when it does not happen keeps moving it back. What is interesting is that when these predictions fail, it does not appear to damage the author's reputation. They continue to write books of prophecy, which sell very well indeed. The belief in the rapture is so deeply held by many evangelicals that they continue to believe in it regardless of failed prophecies. Early on, I did as well. I understand. There is an intense fear of "being left behind" as evidenced by the series of best-selling books by that title.

As for me, I had bought into the predictions of the second coming of Christ, the rise of the antichrist, and the Battle of Armageddon totally, and that these events would take place perhaps in the 1970's, but for sure no later than the 1980's. When by 1988 these events had not happened, I became very cynical. I was not going to be "tricked" into making that error of judgment again. No longer would I listen to well-meaning pastors and their arrogant predictions and interpretations of scripture, nor read books that present such judgments that no one can know or that common sense, experience, and observations clearly contradict. So, today when I see Hal Lindsey or others on television still preaching their end-times predictions, I must admit tears often come as I think about the damage they are doing to gullible individuals (as I was) all the while they often live a luxurious life benefiting from the financial contributions of their followers. It still hurts!!

Since much of the end-times theology comes from the book of Revelation, it is interesting to read Elaine Pagels' book on Revelations (2012) in which she describes that for 2000 years its language and images have been used by many persons and institutions to demonize their enemies. What is especially interesting is that when the New Testament was being formed, most lists of books left out Revelation and that it was the emperor Constantine who was influential in having it become a part of the New Testament.

O'Murchu said what I have been thinking about for a long time. "Reflective Christians," he writes, with a maturing faith view the speculation of the end of the world "as preposterous scare-mongering, valuable in earlier times to make sense out of intense suffering and persecution, but today an empty rhetoric based on irrational fear, thriving on human insecurity, alienating more reflective people." (p. 66) But, then I wonder...is the whole theology of the rapture and the punishment for those left behind part of an "ethnic cleansing" idea of the world? Is it a belief that God will once and for all "ethnically cleanse" everyone who does not believe like me? I wonder, "Is the Bible really the 'Word of God' to be taken literally"? By the 1990's, as I entered my fifth decade of life, I began to have great doubts.

Note: *I recognize that individuals have different interpretations of the rapture and the second coming of Jesus and I am purposely avoiding that debate.*

For wide is the gate and broad is the road that leads to destruction, and many enter through it. But small is the gate and narrow the road that leads to life, and only a few find it.

(Matthew 7:13-14)

Chapter Four

WE/THEY: AN APOCALYPTIC VIEW OF THE WORLD

The home and culture in which I was raised was a "we/they" world. We were the good guys…they were the bad guys…and there were lots of bad guys; evil was everywhere. We were the saved, the redeemed, the born again, those separated from the world, and we were the ones who had the right belief system and followed the right practices. We attended the right church…an independent Pentecostal church that believed in the "full gospel" message. They were the non-believers; the atheists, agnostics, the Catholics, Lutherans, Unitarians, and most all the other religions, Christian or otherwise, who did not believe like we did. They were the ones who went to movies, dances, smoked, drank alcohol, and whose women wore make-up. They were the ones who were causing all the problems in the world. If only they'd get "born again!" I was the only child, other than my brothers and sisters, who, from the schools I attended, went to my church. So, all my friends and teachers were part of the "they" crowd, evil persons destined for hell.

The authority used to justify such beliefs and practices was the "Word of God," i.e., the Bible. The Bible was to be taken literally, 100% of the time. It was without error. When asked, "Why are we so few and they so many?" the justification for our small number would come from the Bible, "For wide is the gate and broad is the road that leads to destruction, and many enter through it. But small is the gate and narrow the road that leads to life, and only a few find it." (Matthew 7:13-14) We had found the truth that others had not. We were the good guys.

But yet, as I went through school, I made many friends, liked and respected my teachers, and always struggled with the question; how can we be so sure we are correct and all others are wrong? Is not that actually pride and arrogance? Yet, who was I, a school boy, to argue with the "Word of God," and those in authority from our church to interpret the "Word of God"? These concerns, while repressed at the time, were planted and would come back later in life.

How sad it is that the we/they mentality has moved into the acceptance of "who is a Christian" in our national politics. Despite President Obama's many statements on his acceptance of Christ and his Christian commitment, many still do not believe he is a Christian. In a survey conducted in March of 2012, 52% of Republicans in Mississippi and 45% in Alabama said Obama was a Muslim. (Jackson, *USA Today*) Because of the Mormon faith of Mitt Romney, many also do not accept him as a Christian. If you don't believe just like us or at least very close to us, you are not one of us; you are one of them.

On a deeper note, the idea of "we/they" comes from the apocalyptic view of the world where there is a cosmic battle going on between the forces of God and his angels and the devil and his demons. This view holds that the devil has been given temporary control of the earth, but someday God will defeat him in a major catastrophic battle and God's special followers will "rule and reign" with God on earth. The "we" are those few special born-again people. The vast majority of humans will be sent to hell to burn forever.

In *If Grace is True*, Gulley and Mulholland discuss the "we/they" concept. They write that perhaps the greatest sin people commit, is the arrogance that we have the truth and others don't—that we will be saved and others won't. We go to heaven and others are dammed. Our God is pleased with us and not with others. If others don't accept our God, since they are dammed anyway, we can treat them harshly. (pp. 157-159)

Carlton Pearson writes, "Our culture's obsession with the return of Christ and the end of the world is bleeding Christianity dry of relevance, respect, and any ability to focus on what should be its true mission; uniting all the children of God as a single people for peace, health and hope, and joyful anticipation of good." (2010, p. 72) "If you want to see born-again Christians become truly animated, just mention the rapture and Armageddon to them...I've seen mellow believers get a fire in their eyes...to leave the rest of humanity behind for the tribulation...I think that this enthusiasm represents the true cancer that is eating away at modern Christian tradition...the zeal for judgment day is essentially a nihilistic expression of passion for death and destruction and a hatred for the world because the Christian believer doesn't think it will happen to him." (p. 74) "It is built on the division between God and devil, good and evil...there is us and the other...we are an armed camp of the elect few who see the truth...we'll be taken away...everyone else is damned." (p. 80) His admonition on end times theology is that "It is essential that we do not delude ourselves into thinking we know the mind of God or the nature of the divine plan for each event in the world." (p. 84)

This apocalyptic view largely comes from a few books of the Bible, including but not limited to Daniel and Revelation. If a person has this view, it significantly affects his/her analysis of world events. All the events that happen on this earth are seen through this lens. A major influence in our relationship and support for Israel comes from this world view. This world view contributes to some being opposed to working within the United Nations and any support for the European Common Market since some believe that end-times prophecies speak against these institutions. And it certainly contributes to opposition to gay rights and abortion.

When a major natural disaster occurs, those with an apocalyptic world view will read into it either the action of God or the action of the devil. When hurricane Katrina slammed into New Orleans, a number of televangelists claimed that it was God's punishment of

New Orleans because of its sin and our nation allowing gay rights. When the great oil spill of 2010 in the Gulf of Mexico occurred, again televangelists were quick to point out that it was caused by God in response to the USA indicating our lack of support for Israel. When Haiti had such a terrible earthquake, a televangelist indicated it was God's punishment for Haiti making a "pact with the devil." When the 2011 earthquake hit Virginia and a possible crack resulted in the Washington Monument, it was a sign of the end times according to the same televangelists. When a Hurricane caused flooding in the Northeast a few weeks after the Virginia earthquake, a prominent presidential candidate indicated that perhaps God was sending a message to Washington.

It is reminiscent of the time of the Old Testament writers. Volcanic eruptions were attributed to God sending fire to destroy a city. The earth was flat with a supernatural being living above in the sky. Terrible things came out of the sky…tornadoes, rain and hail storms, hurricanes, clouds often covered the mountains, and at times the oceans roared with great waves (tsunamis) and the earth bellowed with fire (volcanoes). God in the skies seemed to often be angry with earth as He sent all kinds of devastation. The people of ancient times developed numerous rituals and practices, including human and animal sacrifices, to please God so he would not send these calamities. When clouds were on the mountains with a thunderstorm, the writers claimed that God was on the mountain. Emperors were often given the title "Son of God" and births of great leaders were often described as supernatural.

It seems as if those with an apocalyptic view of the world are living with a view of the world from over 2000 years ago when it was believed the earth was the center of the universe and God ruled in the heavens above the earth. This view of the world and universe has been overwhelmingly rejected as we discover the expansive and expanding nature of our universe and the extremely small part the planet Earth plays in it. It is said that "ignorance is bliss," however, it has also been said that nothing is more dangerous than "arrogant ignorance." In my opinion, being born and raised in an environment of "we/they" with an apocalyptic world view is very dangerous. And when leaders in a country are influenced by such belief systems, decisions made can be devastating for that country.

When President Obama gave his Middle East speech in 2010, he emphasized the need for a compromise between Israel and Palestine in order to achieve peace. Netanyahu, evangelicals, and politicians who want to appease evangelical voters, quickly denounced any potential compromise since evangelicals believe that because God gave a specific piece of land to Israel 3500 years ago, there can be no compromise, no peace, no accommodation. It is interesting to note that Israel took the land 3500 years ago by force, according to the Biblical account, and killed all men, women, and children who lived there since God told them to do so. Moreover, they also re-took the land by force in 1948 and displaced tens of thousands of individuals that had lived there for over 1000 years.

As long as individuals consider the Bible to be the literal Word of God, there is really little hope for peace or compromise between Israel and the rest of the Middle East nor between evangelical Christians and anyone who does not believe as they do. As noted by Karen Armstrong (2000), the greatest threat to peace in the world is the radical beliefs of some Christians, Muslims, and Jews. While religion has so much to offer, what a sad state of affairs the radicalization of religions produces. It all begins when followers of a belief system consider their sacred books, often written thousands of years ago, in a different time, for a different culture, and for a different people, as the Word of God to be followed exactly as written. This belief system can lead to deadly results.

Men never do evil so completely and cheerfully as when they do it from religious conviction.

—Blaise Pascal

Chapter Five

VIOLENCE AND THE FOUNDING
OF ANCIENT ISRAEL

During my lifetime the world has witnessed the horror of brutality. Specifically appalling is the ethnic cleansing that has taken place in a multitude of settings in the 20th century. It is inconceivable how the German people, led by Hitler, could plan and implement the killing of more than 6 million Jews. Their goal was to exterminate the Jews.

In the 1970's in Cambodia more than 200,000 people were executed by the Khmer Rouge with an additional estimate of 2 million people dying from starvation and disease. In the 1990's we learned that Serbs in Kosovo carried out an organized campaign to drive ethnic Albanians out of Kosovo, killing or deporting nearly 800,000. In 1994, the Hutu in Rwanda went on a 100-day killing spree to exterminate the minority Tutsi population. Close to one million Tutsi's were killed in this 100-day period alone.

The modern world has been appalled by these mass killings. Upon the ending of World War II, war trials were held and many Germans who were involved in the killing of the Jews were tried, found guilty, and executed. Again, the world did not accept such ethnic cleansing in Cambodia, Kosovo, and Rwanda, and several of the leaders of the carnage were eventually tried and convicted.

But ethnic cleansing is not a new concept. It even appears to be sanctioned by the God of the Bible. As I grew up studying the Old Testament, I read about numerous examples of ethnic cleansing and brutality. However, somehow I overlooked them and was not outraged. Considering our current anger over the ethnic cleansing we have seen in our generation, why have we ignored such behavior found in the Old Testament? Was it because it was done by the children of Israel and hence acceptable? Did we accept the scriptures that indicated that the God of Israel had ordered it and thus it was OK?

First, the book of Genesis records that God specifically chose Abraham and told him "I will bless you, I will make your name great." (Genesis 12:2) It records that while traveling through a certain country where the Canaanites were living; the Lord appeared to Abram and said, "to your offspring, I will give this land." (Genesis 12:6-7) And, then to further describe the land God would give to Israel, the Bible records that the Lord said, "To your descendants I give this land, from the river of Egypt to the great river, the Euphrates—the land of the Kenites, Kenizzites, Kadmonites, Hittites, Perizzites, Rephaites, Amorites, Canaanites, Girgashites, and Jebusites." (Genesis 15:18-21) The promise was confirmed to Jacob in Genesis 28 and to Moses in Exodus Chapter 23. It is extremely important to note that the land the Bible reports that God is giving to Abraham and his offspring was already inhabited by other people. Someone else possessed the land! It raises the question, "Why is God giving to the descendants of Abraham a land where other people live?" Does this story accurately describe the nature and character of God? Did this really happen as described in the Bible?

Second, there comes a period in history when the Bible records that it is time for Abraham's descendants to take the land. After 400 years in slavery in Egypt and 40 years wandering in the desert, the time has come. The book of Exodus describes the process of taking possession of the land. "My angel will go ahead of you and bring you into the land of the Amorites, Hittites, Perizzites, Canaanites, Hivites, and Jebusites, and I will wipe them out." (Exodus 23:23) God tells Moses, "Break camp and advance into the hill country of the Amorites; go to all the neighboring peoples in the Arabah, in the mountains, in the western foothills, in the Negev and along the coast, to the land of the Canaanites and to Lebanon, as far as the great river, the Euphrates. See, I have given you this land. Go in and take possession of the land that the Lord swore he would give to your fathers—to Abraham, Isaac and Jacob—and to their descendants after them." (Deuteronomy 1:7-8) Again, it does not seem to matter to the God of the Bible that other people possessed the land. God orders his chosen people to take it!

Third, the Bible records that taking possession of the land God gave them was a bloody, violent affair. Joshua led Israel to conquer the land of Canaan. He went from city to city and "carried off for themselves all the plunder and livestock of these cities, but all the people they put to the sword until they completely destroyed them, not sparing anyone that breathed as the Lord commanded his servant Moses, so Moses commanded Joshua, and Joshua did it." (Joshua 11:14) "Exterminating them without mercy, as the Lord had commanded." (Joshua 11:20) Not unlike the holocaust in Germany, the killing fields of Cambodia, and the ethnic cleansing in Kosovo and Rwanda. Did God really order these atrocities? Are these events as recorded in the Bible true?

After the Israelites were freed of their captivity in Egypt, God tells them to attack King Sihon of Heshbon. Faithfully, they "put to death everyone in the cities, men, women, and dependents" and "left no survivor." (Deuteronomy 2:31-34) Again, they are commanded to do the same to King Og of Bashan. The Israelites "slaughtered them and left no survivor." (Deuteronomy 3:1-7) In resettling the Promised Land, they are commanded by God to take the land of seven nations and "not leave any creature alive. You shall annihilate them." (Deuteronomy 7:1-6; 20:16-17) Can we imagine this behavior being accepted in the 21th century? Did this really happen as written in the Bible...ordered by God and carried out by the Israelites?

Joshua's army attacked Jericho and "put everyone to the sword, men and women, young and old." (Joshua 6:20-21) Later, the Lord told Joshua to do the same to the people of Ai. (Joshua 8:1-2) In obedience to God's commands, Joshua's army did the same to many other cities. If the stories in the Bible are true, tens of thousands of men, women, and children were exterminated in this take-over of the Promised Land. The book of Psalms describes these massacres as proof that the Lord's "love endures forever." (Psalms 136:17-21) Is this Biblical account really true? Does this describe the nature of God?

According to the Bible, all of the carnage was ordered by God. God ordered the Israelites to make war on Midian and they killed all the men and burned their cities. (Numbers 31:7-12) However, Moses was angry, because they did not kill the women and children. So he ordered the soldiers to "kill every male dependent, and kill every woman who has had intercourse with a man, but spare for yourselves every woman among them who has not had intercourse." (Numbers 31:14-18) God gave Moses commands how to give the captive virgins to the fighting men and the community. (Numbers 31:25-47) Just take a moment and think about this story. Is this accurate? Is this what God would actually order?

The book of Joshua records the battles and the bloody conquest of the Promised Land. In Chapters 11 and 12, it is recorded that "Joshua took this entire land...He captured all their kings and struck them down, putting them to death...31 kings in all." (Joshua 11:16-17; 12:24) The last chapter of Joshua reports that "I gave you a land on which you did not toil and cities you did not build; and you live in them and eat from vineyards and olive groves that you did not plant." (Joshua 24:13) The taking of the land seems to be complete with the previous residents of that land killed or driven out. If the Bible is to be accepted as the Word of God, literally and without error, the conquest of the Promised Land by the Israelites was accomplished under the direction of God and resulted in the killing of perhaps millions of men, women, and children. Isn't there something wrong with this story?

After the land was conquered, the killing did not stop because there was a chance that all the previous residents had not been completely eliminated. On orders from God, the prophet Samuel told Saul: "Go now and fall upon the Amalekites and destroy them.... Spare no one; put them all to death, men and women, children and babes in arms, herds and flocks, camels and asses." (I Samuel 15:1-3) Isaiah describes God's anger against Babylon: "All who are found will be stabbed, all who are taken will fall by the sword; their infants will be dashed to the ground before their eyes." (Isaiah 13:1-20) Jeremiah declares "A curse on him who is slack in doing the Lord's work! A curse on him who withholds his sword from bloodshed!" (Jeremiah 48:10) Is this really the "Lord's work" commanded by God to kill all those who disagree with you?

It is interesting to observe the events today regarding Israel and its relationships with its neighbors. Evangelical Christians believe that since God gave a specific piece of land to Israel, there can be no compromise. What is overlooked is that over 3500 years ago Israel took the land by force slaughtering most of the inhabitants. Is it any wonder why there is no peace in this land?

We read chapter after chapter of ethnic cleansing in the Old Testament seemingly sanctioned and commanded by God. How can we read this today without outrage? How can we believe that the God of Jesus would order such killings? How can we accept the literal interpretation of these scriptures? Sure, we've heard the actions being justified such as, God wanted to protect Israel from the influence of the ungodly so the ungodly needed to be eliminated; "do not let them live in your land, or they will cause you to sin against me." (Exodus

23:33) If God is all knowing, he should have known the ethnic cleansing really would not accomplish that goal.

Would God grant title of the land to Abraham's descendants knowing that the occupants would need to be killed? Perhaps God never gave this piece of land to Abraham and his descendants. Perhaps God never gave orders to kill anyone. Perhaps men in their hunger for power used the name of God to accomplish their own purposes. Maybe we need to read the Bible from a different perspective. Maybe it is not the inerrant, literal Word of God.

I am reminded of my 14 years on the faculty and in administrative positions at Oral Roberts University. Often Oral Roberts claimed that the Lord had directly spoken to him about things he was supposed to do. Most famously, God gave him orders to build the City of Faith, a giant 60-story medical clinic, a 30-story hospital, and a 20-story research building, and through these endeavors the healing power of God would reach many people. He was also to add to his undergraduate institution a medical school, a dental school, and a law school. I saw in Roberts a person who wanted at "all cost" to accomplish what he felt was his calling. When God spoke to Oral, everyone was to "jump" and certainly not question. Many consultants and advisors recommended to Roberts not to take on this huge challenge. Roberts would not listen to anyone who gave him contrary advice. Yes, the medical, dental, and law schools opened their doors and accepted students and the 110 stories of buildings were built. However, despite Roberts' pleas that "God would kill him" if he did not raise the money to build all that God had commanded him to do, within 10 years the medical, dental, and law schools were closed, faculty members lost their jobs, and the 110 stories of buildings were an empty shell. Roberts lived another 24 years and died at the age of 92. Perhaps God had not told Oral Roberts to build such an institution.

Unfortunately, I heard many of the charismatic/evangelical speakers that would come to ORU also tell us of the special messages they had received from God. It seemed as though God spoke regularly to these evangelists. Maybe what happened at ORU occurred in the Old Testament as well. Perhaps powerful individuals "used God" to accomplish their own personal agendas. As with the leaders of old, I witnessed how Roberts became a wealthy man from the gifts of his partners (contributors), and I saw some of his partners give almost everything they had in hopes of receiving healing and/or wealth.

The Biblical stories of the violence by which the children of Israel took the Promised Land some 3500 years ago lead me to one of two conclusions: (1) Accept the account as the accurate Word of God. If this is correct then God is sadistic and violent; He is an angry God who orders ethnic cleansing, selects one group of his creation and rejects others. Since the Bible records that God has committed or ordered many violent acts, it could be argued that God's followers today may decide they can behave likewise. (2) Reject these stories of God giving a certain piece of land to the descendants of Abraham and the violence by which God ordered them to take it. Rejection of God's role in these stories as "truth" results in one not accepting the Bible being the literal and inerrant Word of God. Perhaps these are man's account of what happened. Perhaps man in his thrust for power told the people that God had told him to do all these violent things.

Mesle expresses it this way; "we easily mistake our own desires for God's." It was easy to believe that God had granted them their own desire for the land of Canaan that allowed them to slaughter the inhabitants. Those who accept the literal interpretation of the Bible accept the killing as justified. I agree with Mesle when he says, "Personally, I don't want to be around people who are so rigidly sure of their religious and moral infallibility that they can approve the slaughtering of innocent children in the name of love. Dogmatism is dangerous." (p. 87-92)

Perhaps Borg says it the best. The stories in the Bible of Israel conquering the Promised Land is not God's story of the events, rather the stories are Israel's account of the events. It is a very human story written by men and not God's written word. (*The Heart of Christianity*, p. 52)

"*I know of no book which has been a source of brutality and sadistic conduct, both public and private, that can compare with the Bible.*

—Sir James Paget

Chapter Six

VIOLENCE IN THE BIBLE
AS PUNISHMENT

Violent messages abound in television, movies, video games, and the internet. Violence seems to be encouraged in response to fear and problems. While it is understandable that people are apprehensive about possible effects of violence in entertainment, it is unclear why very few evangelical Christians are disturbed by the widespread promotion of violence in the Bible. It has been reported that there are over 1000 references to violence in the Bible that were either caused or ordered by God. Two especially dramatic examples are where the Bible says that God damned the entire human race because of the acts of the first two people. (Genesis 3:16-23; Romans 5:18) The Bible also records that God caused a worldwide flood that killed every living creature. (Genesis 7:20-23)

Further examples of the violence narrative from the New Testament record that God required the killing of his own son. (Romans 3:24-25) It promises God will send to eternal punishment all who do not accept Jesus. (Revelations 21:8) Taking many of the Bible's stories literally illustrates God's methods of tormenting and killing people. Sommers (*Violence and the Biblical God*) writes that God's frequent resorting to violence makes God appear to be a sociopathic mass murderer. How does this characterization of God compare to a loving, caring image of Jesus? Violent religious examples, presented in sacred scriptural texts, perhaps are as likely to influence people to behave violently as what is seen in the mass media.

It is interesting to observe that while the Bible indicates that God is perfect (Psalms 18:30), just (Isaiah 30:18), compassionate (Psalms 86:15), merciful (Deuteronomy 4:31), and loving (I John 4:9, 16), the

Bible also records that God has committed or ordered many violent acts. So, it could be argued that although God is said to possess commendable characteristics but still commits or orders violence, his followers may decide they can behave likewise and still be good people. They might even think they have a religious obligation to follow his violent pattern. The American patriot Thomas Paine referred to such attitudes when he said, "The belief in a cruel god makes a cruel man." (Ingersoll, p. 483)

In the previous section I outlined the often gratuitous violence in the founding of ancient Israel. The Bible goes on to record God's determination to punish his children severely if they do not obey him. God inflicts diseases on people. After the Exodus from Egypt, the Israelites complained about having no meat to eat while wandering in the wilderness. Then the "Lord's anger broke out against the people and he struck them with a deadly plague." (Numbers 11:4-6; 33-34) Not having learned their lesson, the people later complained about the leadership of Moses and Aaron. So God sent a plague that killed 14,700 more of them. (Numbers 16:41-50)

The Bible reports that God used a plague to kill 24,000 Israelites because they had worshiped the gods of the Midianites. This plague was stopped only when Phinehas, after seeing an Israelite man take a Midianite woman into the man's family, put his spear through both of them together. (Numbers 25:1-9) God praised Phinehas and rewarded him for the act. (Numbers 25:10-15)

The God described in the Bible used the same punishment on subsequent generations. He sent a pestilence that killed 70,000 men because King David took a census. (I Chronicles 21:1:7-15) After King Uzziah of Judah offended the Lord by burning incense in the temple, God struck him with leprosy so that "King Uzziah had leprosy until the day he died." (II Chronicles 26:16-21)

According to the Bible, God forewarned his prophets of similar divine retribution if his people persist in disobedience. He revealed to Jeremiah his intent to "strike down those who live in this city, both men and animals—and they will die of a terrible plague." (Jeremiah 21:3-7) The prophet Ezekiel said that because Jerusalem had not followed God's ways, it would be consumed "without pity" and a third of the people "will die of the plague." (Ezekiel 5:11-12) Ezekiel claims that God appointed men to punish Jerusalem for its "abominations." The Lord told them to "kill without showing pity or compassion. Slaughter old men, young men and maidens, women, and children." (Ezekiel 9:1-7)

In II Chronicles, there is another report of the Lord's anger breaking out against Jerusalem. This time he "brought up against them the king of the Babylonians, who killed their young men with the sword...and spared neither young man nor young maiden, old man or aged." (II Chronicles 36:16-17)

After the Israelites disobeyed God's commandments and worshipped other gods, the "Lord rejected all the people of Israel; he afflicted them and gave them into the hands of plunderers, until he thrust them from his presence." (II Kings 17:19-20) Later, God said about Judah: "They will be looted and plundered by all their foes, because they have done evil in my eyes and provoked me to anger." (II Kings 21:14-15) Jeremiah gives the following message from the Lord: "See, I will send venomous snakes among you, vipers that cannot be charmed and they will bite you declares the Lord." (Jeremiah 8:17) Jeremiah says the Almighty will hand the people of Judah to the king of Babylon, who will take their wealth, deport them to Babylon, or put them to the sword. (Jeremiah 20:4-5) In the same book, the Lord declares, "At midday I will bring a destroyer against the mothers of their young men; suddenly I will bring down on them anguish and terror." (Jeremiah 15:8-9)

The Bible says that God used famines to torment and kill people.

After David angered God by taking the census, God said one of the punishments David could choose was 3 years of famine. (I Chronicles 21:7-12) Jeremiah says God promised to make an end to the people of Judah by "sword, with famine and plague." (Jeremiah 14:12) According to Ezekiel, God vowed to spend his anger on Israel by causing men to fall by sword, famine, and plague. (Ezekiel 6:11-12)

The Bible reports that God uses fire on people. There is the story of God raining fire and brimstone on the cities of Sodom and Gomorrah. By this means, he "overthrew those cities and the entire plain, including all those living in the cities." (Genesis 19:24-25) Similar punishment was dealt to two of Aaron's sons, who presented "illicit fire" before the Lord. In response: "Fire came out from the presence of the Lord and consumed them; and so they died before the Lord." (Leviticus 10:1-2) After several Israelites led 250 men in rebellion against Moses' authority, "fire came out from the Lord and consumed the 250 men." (Numbers 16:1-2; 31-35) God ordered his people to use fire as a punishment. The Law of Moses states that if the daughter of a priest becomes a prostitute, she must be burned in the fire. (Leviticus 21:9)

According to the Bible, the killing of babies is another way God would express his anger. As already noted, babies were drowned in the worldwide flood, Egyptian babies were among the firstborn killed at the Passover, and babies were killed in the wars of extermination. After King David succeeded in having a loyal Israeli soldier, Uriah, killed in battle and taking his wife, Bathsheba, the punishment of David is killing the baby. (II Samuel 12:7-18) Isaiah says a similar punishment would be used against the Babylonians. He quotes the Lord as vowing that "infants will be dashed to pieces before their eyes.... I will stir up against them the Medes...who have no mercy on infants, nor will they look with compassion on children." (Isaiah 13:15-18) The book of Psalms indicates that those inflicting this punishment can enjoy it. The book says about Babylon: "Happy is he who seizes your infants and dashes them against the rocks." (Psalms 137:8-9)

The Bible is a major proponent of capital punishment, even for trivial offenses. After the Israelites found a man gathering sticks on the Sabbath, the Lord said, "The man must die; the whole assembly must stone him outside the camp." (Numbers 15:32-36) God ordered the death penalty for anyone else who works on the Sabbath. (Exodus 31:14-15) People were not to spare even their children from execution. God prescribed capital punishment for reviling one's father and mother. (Leviticus 20:9) And as for a son who is disobedient and out of control, the Lord directed that "all the men of the town shall stone him to death. You must purge this evil from among you." (Deuteronomy 21:18-21) The Law of Moses requires the death penalty for other acts, too. They include adultery, (Leviticus 20:10) and homosexuality. (Leviticus 20:13)

According to the book of Leviticus, God promises that if the Israelites disobey him: "I myself will punish you for your sins seven times over. You will eat the flesh of your sons and the flesh of your daughters." (Leviticus 26:27-29) Isaiah describes a punishment of Israel: "On the right they will devour, but still be hungry; on the left they will eat, but not be satisfied. Each will feed on the flesh of his own offspring." (Isaiah 9:20) Jeremiah says the Lord promised to punish Jerusalem by "devastating this city and make it an object of scorn; all who pass by will be appalled and will scoff because of all its wounds. I will make them eat the flesh of their sons and daughters, and they will eat one another's flesh during the stress of the siege imposed on them by the enemies who seek their lives." (Jeremiah 19:8-9) After reading these verses, how can any rational, thinking person believe the Bible is the Word of God to be taken literally?

The Old Testament supports an "eye for an eye" retribution. "If anyone injures his neighbor, whatever he has done must be done to him: fracture for fracture, eye for eye, tooth for tooth. As he has injured the other, so he is to be injured." (Leviticus 24:19-20) And the Lord specified that in administering this punishment, "Show no pity." (Deuteronomy 19:21)

Does the Bible condone human sacrifice? God commended Abraham for being willing to sacrifice his son Isaac. Fortunately for Isaac, an angel stayed Abraham's knife-wielding hand at the last second. (Genesis 22:10-12) The daughter of Jephthah was not so lucky. Jephthah sacrificed her to fulfill a vow he had made to the Lord. (Judges 11:29-40) In the New Testament, Jephthah is listed as one of the great men of faith. (Hebrews 11:32) The God of the New Testament also showed support for human sacrifice by having it done to his son. (Romans 3:24-25)

The New Testament's depiction of God is hardly more favorable. The book of Revelation states that in the end times, heavenly power and a sword will be given to a rider on a horse. He will be allowed to make men slaughter one another. (Revelation 6:3-4) Another rider will be granted similar divine authority, including power to kill with the sword over a quarter of the earth. (Revelation 6:7-8) Later, four angels and their cavalry of 200 million will go forth to slay a third of mankind. (Revelation 9:14-16) This destruction is preliminary to Christ himself coming on a white horse, leading the armies of heaven. A sharp sword will extend from his mouth to smite the nations, whose armies will be killed by the sword. (Revelation 19:11-21) While some understand these passages as metaphor, if one believes the Bible is to be taken literally, then this is not a metaphor, rather a factual depiction of what is to come.

It is interesting to note that this violence as a form of punishment was ineffective. Through the prophet Amos, the Lord complained to his people that although he had "sent plagues among you as I did to

Egypt," they still did not return to him. (Amos 4:10) Nevertheless, the New Testament shows that God will continue the same behavior. The book of Revelation states that one of the four horsemen of the Apocalypse will be given power over a quarter of the earth, including power to kill by pestilence. (Revelation 6:8)

As was true with pestilence, the God of the New Testament intends to continue using famine as punishment. The book of Revelation claims that the third of the 4 horsemen of the Apocalypse will be given divine authority to cause famine on earth. (Revelation 6:5-6)

In describing the end times, the book of Revelation reports that after an angel blows a trumpet, fire mingled with blood will be cast upon the earth. This will result in a third of the earth being burnt. (Revelation 8:7) Many verses in Revelation also report fire will be a part of the final judgment in many verses. (Revelation 9, 11, 16, 18 and 20) Because eternal torture in hell is the most horrible punishment imaginable, the Bible has succeeded in reaching the pinnacle of viciousness and mercilessness.

These Bible verses report many violent, brutal, and heartless acts that appear to be supported and approved by God, which leads one to question whether the Bible should be discredited as a moral guide. Thomas Paine said: "To read the Bible without horror, we must undo everything that is tender, sympathizing and benevolent in the heart of man." (Ingersoll, p. 482) The Biblical God's behavior has been considered a model of goodness and justice. Throughout history, innumerable Bible-believers have followed his example and teachings by committing horrendous violence—and felt good about themselves for doing so. Such acts led Sir James Paget to say in the nineteenth century: "I know of no book which has been a source of brutality and sadistic conduct, both public and private, that can compare with the Bible." (Haught, p. 181) And the Enlightenment philosopher

Montesquieu observed: "No kingdom has ever suffered as many civil wars as the kingdom of Christ." (p. 50)

As Christians and Americans, we have been appalled by what we understand of the Islamic teaching of putting to death "infidels." However, it is not only the Koran that teaches such intolerance. The Old Testament also orders the putting to death of "infidels" if we are to take the command of God found in Deuteronomy 13 to be factual and to be followed. "If your very own brother, or your son or daughter, or the wife you love, or your closest friend secretly entices you, saying 'let us go and worship other gods'…do not yield to him or listen to him. Show him no pity. Do not spare him or shield him. You must certainly put him to death." (v. 6-9) "If you hear it said about one of the towns…men have arisen among you and have led the people of the town astray, saying 'let us go and worship other gods'…you must certainly put to the sword all the people that live in that town. Destroy it completely…completely burn the town…as a whole burnt offering to the Lord your God." (v. 12-16)

If one pays homage to another god "they shall be utterly destroyed." (Exodus 22:20, NAS). "If anyone curses his God, he will be held responsible; anyone who blasphemes the name of the Lord must be put to death." (Leviticus 24:15-16) Again, in chapter 17 of Deuteronomy, if a person worships other gods they shall "stone that person to death." (v. 2-6) These scriptures show absolutely no tolerance for anyone who does not believe and worship exactly as ordered by the law of the "church" of their day.

I note that most western Christians do not appear to be following these commandments of God as found in the Bible. Are these passages that most Christians have "left behind"? Apparently so, and thank God for that. However, the question must be raised, if the Bible is accepted as the Word of God, why have evangelical Christians disregarded these commandments? Do Christians who claim the Bible is the Word of God to be taken literally actually practice it? Do Christians who claim Biblical inerrancy actually practice selective literality; that is, where the Bible supports their belief system, they claim it to be literally true; however, where the Bible does not support their belief system, they will conveniently ignore those verses or find excuses to pay no heed to them? If a person genuinely believes the Bible is the Word of God, then all of God's decrees must be followed since there really is no middle ground. How can a person living in the 21st Century believe that the Bible (as well as the sacred texts of other religions) is the written Word of God, totally true, to be accepted completely and to be followed today? Christians need to leave behind the literal interpretation of the Bible and reconsider if it is the "Word of God."

Note: *Some of the information for this and the previous section was adapted from Sommer, Joseph. "Violence and the Biblical God". http://www.humanismbyjoe.co/violence-and-the-biblical-god/. Accessed June 30, 2012.*

Slavery is a blessing, both to the master and to the slave, and that it is an ordinance of God...established from the Bible, and, as such, must continue till the end of time.

—J. B. Thrasher 1860

Chapter Seven

SLAVERY AND DISCRIMINATION
AGAINST HOMOSEXUALS

Are we to accept slavery, as referenced in the Bible? When Ham, the son of Noah and the father of Canaan, (see Genesis 9) saw his father's nakedness (after he became drunk with wine…but that's another story), he was cursed, and his punishment was to be a slave to his brothers. Since some think that Canaan migrated to Africa, this passage has been used by Christians as justification for the enslavement of the blacks. Scriptures provide evidence that the Bible does not condemn slavery; rather, guidelines for the treatment of slaves can be found in Leviticus 25:44-46; Exodus 21:7-11; Ephesians 6:5; and 1 Timothy 6:1-4. Exodus 21:21 states "the slave is his money."

If the Bible condones slavery, should we? If the answer is "no," are we denying sections of the Bible (both Old and New Testament) as the literal Word of God? Two specific examples of Biblical support of slavery can be found in Leviticus 25:44-46 where it states: "Your male and female slaves are to come from the nations around you; from them you may buy slaves…you can will them to your children as inherited property and can make them slaves for life." Exodus 21:20 further defines slaves as property: "If a man beats his male or female slaves with a rod and the slave dies as a direct result, he must be punished, but he is not to be punished if the slave gets up after a day or two, since the slave is his property."

Many in the South believed and accepted this point of view that slaves were property. This was the position of the US Supreme Court prior to the Civil War, and the South and the North went to war at least in part over the Biblical interpretation of slavery. J. B. Thrasher, a leader of the Confederacy, made a widely-supported speech in

1860 on "*Slavery: A Divine Institution.*" (Accessed March 12, 2012) He felt that slavery was a divine institution established by God. In this speech, he quotes widely from the Bible in support of slavery. Referring to the 9th chapter of Genesis, he writes that "Noah, who was inspired of God, cursed his grandson, Canaan, in these words: 'Cursed be Canaan! The lowest of slaves will he be to his brothers.' He also said, 'Blessed be the Lord, the God of Shem! May Canaan be the slave of Shem. May God extend the territory of Japheth, may Japheth live in the tents of Shem, and may Canaan be his slave.'" (Genesis 9: 24-27) Thrasher went on to say that "slavery is a blessing, both to the master and to the slave, and that it is an ordinance of God…established from the Bible, and, as such, must continue till the end of time."

Thrasher further stated, "We find that God has ordained one portion of the human race to be bond slaves, from the period whence nations commenced—and that he has transmitted to us his decrees on the subject, through his inspired writers. That the greater portion of the human race, thus ordained to bond service by Omnipotent decrees…whom we hold in slavery. That the negroes whom we hold in bondage, are the lowest and most degraded of the descendants of Canaan."

And relative to the Civil War he stated, "We, in the South, therefore, believe it to be our duty to God, to ourselves, and to posterity, to perpetuate African slavery, and to extend it as a missionary duty. This can only be done by severing all government relations with the northern states, and forming a southern Confederacy of slave states."

In graduate school, I saw for the first time the discrimination a black friend of mine received from a white professor from Georgia. For the first time I saw real poverty and lived in an area of Springfield, Massachusetts, which was predominately black. I saw first-hand blacks seeking their freedom from oppression and witnessed the bombing of a store a block away from where we lived. I was deeply affected by the assassinations of Bobby Kennedy and Martin Luther King Jr., 2 men trying to promote peace and justice. I began reflecting on the preaching from the church I had heard in my youth that blacks had the curse of Canaan which had allowed slavery and discrimination, and their fate had been the result of that curse found in the Bible.

The acceptance of slavery in the Bible is one more issue that makes me question whether or not the Bible can be the Word of God. Perhaps a better alternative is to re-evaluate whether or not the Bible should be accepted literally, without error, and as the Word of God.

As the Bible was used to discriminate against blacks, I wonder if today the Bible is being used to discriminate against homosexuals. As the Bible was used to develop laws against the freedom for blacks, I wonder if the Bible is being used today to keep or create laws against homosexuals. I note that Jesus said nothing about homosexuality. Perhaps we should follow his example. Perhaps fundamentalism in Christianity is too much like the Pharisees of Jesus' day…too much focus on laws and "right" beliefs and too little focus on loving God and our neighbors.

The anger expressed by evangelical/fundamentalist Christians is often appalling. Nowhere is this more evident than the crusade against homosexuals. In May of 2012 Pastor Charles Worley of Providence Road Baptist Church in Maiden, N.C., called for gays and lesbians to be put in an electrified pen and ultimately killed off. "Build a great, big, large fence and you know what, in a few years, they'll die out!" Worley suggests in a YouTube clip. (*Huffington Post Video*. Accessed June 8, 2012)

I often feel like Anne Rice and want to leave the Christian faith all together. I've not just been "drawn away" but often feel I've been "driven away." It seems like the voices of evangelical Christianity are those of fear, attacking all those who disagree with them, and showing no compassion. I no longer feel at home in that unkindness. The evangelical Christian attack on and rejection of homosexuals is especially offensive.

In 1969 I applied for and received my first research grant. It was funded by the American Heart Association to conduct research on the effects of aerobic exercise on cholesterol. In preparation to conduct the study, I began the process of learning how to accurately measure blood cholesterol. I took blood samples from volunteers including myself. I would draw the blood and then take the sample to the laboratory and measure the cholesterol in the blood. I remember when I measured and analyzed my blood and the results indicated a cholesterol of 326. I thought, "this cannot be!" I was physically fit, had normal body weight, and had a pretty good diet. So, I tested it again and it was about the same. I had tested some unfit, overweight persons whose cholesterol was much lower than mine, and I thought, "that's not fair."

I thought I would change my diet and increase my exercise. For the next 6 months I went on a vegetarian, very low fat diet. Testing my cholesterol again, it had only dropped to 315. Over the next 20 years, I tried every over-the-counter supplement, herb, vitamin, special food, etc. and could never lower my cholesterol below 280. Finally, when nothing else worked and after they had developed safe and effective cholesterol lowering drugs, I began taking a drug, and for the first time in my life, finally at age 50, my cholesterol lowered to below 200. When I was 65, I underwent genetic testing which science had recently discovered, and the specific gene deficiency was identified that caused my high cholesterol. I was born with this abnormality and there was nothing I could do myself to lower it.

At age 35 an electrocardiogram revealed an abnormality (a long QT). The cardiologist told me it was not normal but he did not know its significance. Science studied this issue for years and finally at age 67, testing revealed the specific genetic flaw I had which sometimes caused sudden death. I was happy that it had not happened to me but because of the genetic fault, there was little I could do about it.

A boy we knew who was just in kindergarten passed out in school. A few weeks later it happened again. After many tests and an EEG (Electroencephalogram), a physician informed his parents that the child had a mild form of epilepsy. How devastating that was for them. Why did he have this brain wave abnormality? Apparently, he was born with this problem and there was nothing that could be done about it other than to take medication that helped to minimize the problem. For several years they gave him the medication and he had no fainting spells. After prayer, believing he was healed, they took him off the medication. Within a week, he passed out again and the family finally realized the medication was needed. Some issues are genetic and will never change.

It is interesting to note that in my case, elevated cholesterol did not reveal itself in any outward expression. For epilepsy, that is not true. The Bible talks about individuals "possessed" by the devil and having convulsions. We are thankful that 2000 years later, we understand that epilepsy is caused not by the devil but by brain wave abnormalities.

We have some very good friends who have a 30-year-old daughter with Down syndrome. This is a genetic condition in which a person has 47 chromosomes instead of the normal 46. How does this happen? Extensive research is being conducted to better understand this condition. But, there is nothing the individual with this genetic condition can do to reverse this situation.

Type 1 diabetes (juvenile diabetes) is a disease that occurs when a person is born with a condition where the insulin-producing beta cells in the pancreas are destroyed as the result of an autoimmune disorder. Extensive research has identified a number of gene variants that contribute to this disease. Again, as with genetically elevated cholesterol and Down syndrome, type 1 diabetes is a genetic condition that one is often born with.

Normally, a female has two XX chromosomes and a male has an XY chromosome combination. Any deviation in this normal arrangement will result in some degree of abnormality, some significant and some almost unnoticeable. Studies have shown some males have an extra Y chromosome which results in a XYY chromosome combination and some males have an extra X chromosome which results in a XXY chromosome combination. Some females have an extra X chromosome which results in a XXX chromosome combination and some females are missing the second X chromosome which results in an XO chromosome combination. We do not know why these abnormalities in chromosome combinations happen. Nor do we understand all the ramifications of deviations in sex chromosomes. It is estimated that 10% of the world's population have same-sex preference. Could variations in chromosomes be one possible reason for same-sex preference?

Hubbard and Whitley interviewed individuals who had transitioned from male to female (M2F) or female to male (F2M). (2012) Alejandro describes how he always felt uncomfortable as a male even though he was anatomically a male. He struggled with his identity and finally at age 32 underwent genetic testing and discovered he was XXY, which helped him understand his struggle. Over the next several years, he underwent medical treatment to transition to a female. When the process was completed, he (now she) said that as a female for the first time in her life she felt normal. (p. 203-205)

There are so many conditions that occur over which we have no control. Dwarfism is another one. A couple we know have a son who is 20 years old and is less than 4 feet tall. Both parents are of normal height and he is totally normal in every way except his height. Are he or his parents to blame? Can he do anything about it? Should he be discriminated against because of his height? The answer to these three questions is an emphatic "NO." Research has identified a number of genetic and hormonal causes of dwarfism, most of which are impossible to prevent and difficult to treat medically.

I raise these points to indicate that there is so much being discovered about genes, chromosomes, and the human genome. However, there is also much we still don't know about the make-up of the human organism. If we have so much yet to learn about the anatomy and physiology of the human body, just think about how much there is yet to learn about behavior. How much of behavior might be predetermined by our genetic make-up?

While in Norway in 2010, we toured a leprosy hospital that was still active until the late 1800's. In Biblical times those with leprosy were considered "unclean," were outcasts, and isolated from the rest of the community. Until the 20th Century, those with leprosy were often accused of promiscuity and discriminated against (since they thought the disease might come from sexual activity). Today, we know that leprosy is a disease caused by a bacterium, is treatable, and it is not very contagious.

I am reminded of how in ancient times it was firmly believed that the earth was the center of the universe; it was a truth that was completely accepted until it was discovered that this "truth" was actually false. How difficult it was to accept this new-found truth, especially since entire theological belief systems had been built around the old concept of this truth. Individuals who accepted the new truth were condemned, imprisoned, and could be put to death by the church.

We often make judgments based on erroneous belief systems or incomplete knowledge. This is especially dangerous when we take positions that discriminate against other people based upon our personal belief system. As mentioned previously, for many years we took the rights away from slaves since some people, accepting the literal interpretation of the Bible, believed the Bible supported slavery.

For many years we prohibited women from voting, not least of all, coming from our literal interpretation of the Bible relative to women who were to be "silent in church" (and any other official place), and were to be under male domination. It was not until 1920 that women were allowed to vote in the USA. (As a point of interest, women were allowed to vote in Finland in 1906, Norway in 1913, Denmark in 1915, and Turkey in 1926.)

I have deep concerns that some Christians are using a literal interpretation of the Bible to discriminate against homosexuals. Who among us fully understands the role of genetics and chromosomes in the physiology, anatomy, and behavior of individuals? One milestone study looked at brothers of gay men and found that 52 percent of identical twin brothers were also gay, compared to only 22 percent of non-identical twin brothers. This might indicate the powerful influence of genetics. Scientists are exploring these questions and someday may have the answer. In the meantime, why are those who are taking the rights away from homosexuals so sure that their interpretation of the Bible and of science is the accurate interpretation? Let the person without sin cast the first stone! Bruni (*New York Times*) quotes Jack Drescher, a psychiatrist and psychoanalyst who has written extensively about homosexuality, "most people's sexual attractions are pretty much fixed once they take root." Bruni goes on to say, "there's more wisdom and less harm in accepting and respecting homosexuality than not."

Some rely on Paul's letter to the Romans in Chapter 1 to condemn homosexuality. However, when the entire chapter is read in context, Paul is addressing persons' impure lusts and degrading passions rather than what may occur when two persons of the same sex truly love and care for one another. In her book, *This We Believe: The Christian Case for Gay Civil Rights*, Pearce (2012) writes that of the few (about 5) Biblical references to homosexuality, Biblical scholars indicate that when taken in context, they refer to temple prostitution and other sexual abuses and are not about homosexuality as we describe it today.

If a person decides to use the person's literal interpretation of the Bible to discriminate against homosexuals, then why does the person only selectively apply the verses against homosexuality and allow all other kinds of behavior that the Bible also condemns? If those who do not support rights for homosexuals are honest, they must admit that they selectively take the scriptures on homosexuals and ignore the ones that have been previously discussed:

- Executing the person who works on the Sabbath (Exodus 31:14-15)
- Executing a disobedient child (Leviticus 20:9), (Deuteronomy 21:18-21)
- Executing one who commits adultery (Leviticus 20:10)
- Executing a person who turns away from the faith (Deuteronomy 13:6-9)
- Executing a witch (Exodus 22:18)
- Requiring women to wear long hair and keep their head covered in church (I Corinthians 11:3-16)
- Requiring women to remain silent in church (I Corinthians 14:34-35)
- Prohibiting women from teaching or being in leadership roles over men (1 Timothy 2:11)

In his compelling book, Adams (1996) writes about being raised in a very strict fundamentalist Baptist home and hearing of God's hatred of homosexuals. Growing up, he fought against his attraction to males and lack of attraction to females. From high school he went to Jerry Falwell's Liberty University, prayed for forgiveness, and sought "reparative therapy" to take away his urgings since he was taught that they were sin. To escape, he attempted to take his own life. Finally, before his senior year at Liberty University at age 23, he accepted who he was, a creation of God and loved by God, left Liberty and began an organization to support GLBT students terrorized by fundamentalist Christian institutions. In the process, his family disowned him.

Carey reported in the *New York Times* (May 18, 2012), a prominent retired psychiatrist apologized to the gay community for a decade-old study that concluded some gay people can go straight through what is called reparative therapy. Dr. Robert L. Spitzer, formerly of Columbia University, now says he no longer believes his work showed that. "I believe I owe the gay community an apology for my study making unproven claims of the efficacy of reparative therapy," Spitzer wrote. "I also apologize to any gay person who wasted time and energy undergoing some form of reparative therapy because they believed that I had proven that reparative therapy works."

David Blankenhorn, president of Institute for American Values and the chief witness who testified in favor of California's gay marriage ban during a landmark trial, wrote an opinion piece published in The *New York Times* (Bronner, June 6, 2012) where he said he had changed his mind and said "it's time to accept gay marriage." He went on to write, "As I look at what our society needs most today, I have no stomach for what we often too glibly call 'culture wars.' Especially on this issue, I'm more interested in reconciliation than in further fighting," he said.

Carlton Pearson writes "As has happened throughout history, oppressive regimes find a group or a cause on which to project their own insecurities, fears, and hatreds." (p. 101) Jews, blacks, Catholics, nerds, feminists, homosexuals, etc., have all been groups that have been attacked by one group or another. Today the group evangelicals seem to be going after with a vengeance is homosexuals. A baker in Lakewood, Colorado said he refuses to bake wedding cakes for same-sex marriages since "I'm going to do the best I can to honor Jesus Christ." (*Denver Post.* Sunday, August 05, 2012. p. 3B) There is no evidence from the teachings of Jesus that this decision honors him, rather it seems the opposite of what he teaches.

I reject the discrimination of some churches and individuals against homosexuals and consider it inconsistent with the teachings of Jesus. Such prejudice is a dishonor of Jesus. As has been the thesis of this book, the Bible is not to be taken literally, is certainly not the Word of God, and needs to be interpreted in the context of when it was written. Jesus said nothing about homosexuality. Being Christian, followers of Jesus, his teachings and example take priority over all other scriptures. We need to take seriously his teachings of justice, compassion, and peace.

There is much we don't know about homosexuality. There is much I don't understand. But, when I think about the 50 wonderful years of marriage that Donna and I have had, how can I deny any two men or any two women the joy of being in a loving relationship. How can anyone be so cruel? To selectively accept a literal interpretation of some Biblical passages without understanding the context is indefensible. Let's not wound people because of our ignorance and arrogance.

Thou shalt not suffer a witch to live.

(Exodus 22:18, KJ)

Chapter Eight

TREATMENT OF "WITCHES" AND WOMEN IN THE BIBLE

I was not aware of a terrible practice that is followed in Africa. The Sunday, October 18, 2009 edition of the *Denver Post* reported that children in Africa are increasingly being accused of witchcraft by pastors and then tortured or killed, often by family members. This article was also posted in the *LA Times* and the *Huffington Post*. (Houreld, Accessed October 20, 2009) In the past ten years, over 15,000 children have been charged as witches by pastors of evangelical Christian churches with more than 1000 being tortured and murdered as reviewed by the Associated Press. Thirteen different Christian churches were identified. When problems occur in a family, pastors will accuse the children as being the causes of the problems, pronounce them as witches, and then invoke Exodus 22:18, "Thou shalt not suffer a witch to live." Houreld reported that: "the families are often extremely poor, and sometimes even relieved to have one less mouth to feed." "Poverty, conflict, and poor education lay the foundation for accusations, which are then triggered by the death of a relative, the loss of a job, or the denunciation of a pastor on the make," said Martin Dawes, a spokesman for the United Nations Children's Fund. "When communities come under pressure, they look for scapegoats," he said. "It plays into traditional beliefs that someone is responsible for a negative change...and children are defenseless."

We think of witch-hunt's as being "African" and only practiced by the ignorant. However, the Salem witch-hunt of 1692 that swept through Puritan Massachusetts is among the most infamous events in early American history, and it was not the only such episode to occur in New England. Nineteen persons, primarily women, were hung for being declared to be witches. (Salem Witch Trials)

The Bible also requires that a false prophet be put to death (Deuteronomy 18:20; Zechariah 13:3) as well as anyone accused of being a medium or spiritist. (Leviticus 20:27) If one believes in a literal Bible that is infallible, then one must accept this rather extreme statement since it comes from God. Actually, it also begs the question as to who is a witch. Is a witch a woman who practices magic? If so, then what is magic? Is it praying to gods other than that of the Christian faith? Is it practicing fortune telling? Is it simply being a woman involved in spiritual or healing work or who is a midwife? Is it being someone alleged to have made crops fail or traffic accidents happen? I ask these questions because all these women have been accused and punished for supposed "witchcraft" often with death, as is the Bible's precedent.

It is interesting to observe that most Christians no longer follow some of these passages in the Bible, such as the scriptures related to witches. This leads to the observation that they are actually rejecting the Bible as the literal, inerrant Word of God without admitting it.

What about the Biblical commands relative to women? The more carefully I read the Bible and critically analyze its treatment of women, the more doubtful I become as to its "Word of God" status. If a woman cannot prove on her wedding night that she is a virgin, "she shall be brought to the door of her father's house and there the men of her town shall stone her to death." (Deuteronomy 22:20-21) There is no comparable requirement for a man.

It would appear that the Bible's penalty for rape is pretty weak, and in fact revolting. "If a man happens to meet a virgin who is not pledged to be married and rapes her and they are discovered…he must marry the girl." (Deuteronomy 22:28) That's it? The man must marry the girl and the girl has to accept the man? Is that what the

Word of God says is the penalty for rape? What about the girl? No choice in the matter? This law sounds like a penalty for the non-consenting girl and not the man.

If a woman's husband is in a fight and she comes to help him, the wife better be careful. "If two men are fighting and the wife of one of them comes to rescue her husband from his assailant, and she reaches out and seizes him by his private parts, you shall cut off her hand. Show her no pity." (Deuteronomy 25:11) Is that the Word of God speaking to us? Cut off her hand? Another decree in the Bible says "a woman who is menstruating is unclean and all they touch is unclean." (Leviticus 15:19-32) The definition of unclean in the Old Testament is unsavory. Is this to be taken literally? Is this the Word of God?

Make sure that one's husband never is jealous of his wife since if a man has a "spirit of jealousy," a priest can order the man's wife to drink "water of bitterness," and if she lives she is innocent, but if she dies she was guilty. (Numbers 5:11-31) Is this the "Word of God" as we have been taught? Is this really to be taken literally? Can we selectively decide what we should take literally and what is not literal for our generation and our culture? Or, is the Bible 100% to be taken literally and without error, as the Word of God? If so, then does it not follow that one needs to follow these teachings?

The New Testament continues what many feel is an assault on women. I Corinthians 11:3-16 discusses how a woman must keep her head covered in church and have long hair. Paul's writings state that man was not created for woman but the woman was created for the man. I Corinthians goes on to say that women are to remain silent in church and "are not allowed to speak." (I Corinthians 14:34-35) Consider 1 Timothy 2:11 where Paul says women should not be allowed to teach or to have authority over men. 1 Timothy 2:14-15 blames women for the fall, stating "Adam was not the one deceived, it was the woman" and "women will be saved through childbearing." My goodness, what if a woman does not have children...she won't be saved? Do we really believe that the Bible is to be taken literally, and that it is the Word of God? Can I leave these teachings behind?

While some women were elevated to positions of leadership in the Bible, like Ruth and Esther, and many churches have chosen to leave behind the degrading commandments and teachings relative to women in the Bible, some churches of the 21st century still demonize women. Two of the largest Christian denominations in the USA are the Roman Catholic Church and the Southern Baptist Convention. Both do not allow women to have any authority in the church. The Anglican Church of England in 2012 voted that women cannot be bishops. Unfortunately, accepting the Bible as the Word of God does have significant discriminatory consequences.

Every promise in the book is mine.
Every chapter, every verse, every line.
—A line from a Sunday school song

Chapter Nine

PROMISES IN THE BIBLE

On December 11, 2010, I heard Scott Simon on NPR Radio comment on the death of Elizabeth Edwards. He said, "Elizabeth Edwards lost a son, lost her marriage, got sick, and got scalded in the bright, hot light of fame. But anyone who is a parent will understand: after the death of a child, all other hurts seem small. In 1996, strong winds overturned young Wade Edwards' jeep on a North Carolina highway. He died at the age of sixteen. Nothing overturns your faith in God, fairness, goodness, or makes you ask why you should go on living, more than the death of a child. 'I had to reconcile the God I thought I had with the facts I knew,' Elizabeth Edwards said in recent months. 'I couldn't pray anymore for God to intervene, which means I can't pray for him to intervene in my cancer. Instead, the God that I came to accept promises salvation and enlightenment, and that's the God I live with now. It's not entirely the God I want, but it is the God I believe I have.'"

Elizabeth Edwards expressed what I have been thinking about. Sometimes, the God of the Bible, the God we are taught in our churches, is not the God that seems to exist. Why are we to trust in God? What are we to trust for? As a child I remember singing "Every promise in the book is mine. Every chapter, every verse, every line." Both the Old and New Testaments include many promises. Indeed, I believed that since the Bible was the "Word of God," every promise was mine personally and literally. I remember as a child believing those promises and praying for years for a horse. I never got one. Did God not like me? Or are these promises just childish wishes I needed to "leave behind" as I became an adult?

Over the years, I have come to wonder if these promises can be counted on. I've wondered if these promises are somewhat akin to playing the lottery or slot machines. I don't believe much in playing the lottery or putting money in one-armed bandits (slot machines). But, a few times a year when the lottery gets well into the millions, I'll take perhaps $5 and buy some tickets. When the numbers are posted, I eagerly compare my ticket to the winning numbers and rarely do I even have one of the numbers, let alone a winning ticket. But people do win the lottery! I personally know two persons who have won several million dollars in the lottery; one in Arizona and one in Colorado.

A few times a year I will also play the slot machines. I'll normally take $10 in quarters and put in one quarter at a time, pull the lever, watch the machine spin, and hopefully wait for the spinning to stop and see if I've won anything. What excitement when every once in awhile one or more quarters will drop with a clang into the metal container and I'll pick them up to count my take. Occasionally, I'll play for hours on that original $10 and a few times I've even quit with close to $20 in my pocket. But, the vast majority of times, after less than one hour, my $10 is gone, my hopes dashed, and I'm $10 poorer! (Las Vegas would never get rich off of me because when the $10 is gone, I'm done playing since that is my stop loss limit!)

I sometimes wonder to what extent the promises for us in the Bible are somewhat like buying a lottery ticket or putting money in a one-armed bandit. I'd like to think the odds of my prayers being answered are much better than winning the lottery or having success with the slot machine. I've prayed all my life. I've prayed for guidance when important decisions were to be made and overall, I've made good decisions. I'd like to give credit to God for those good decisions, but I can't say for sure that God was the one that provided the guidance for the decision. I've prayed for success in various endeavors and overall I am thankful for the life I've had. Again, I'd like to thank God for his wonderful love and involvement in my life, but, is it God, or just dumb luck? Being a scientist, I want there to be a direct link between cause and effect and a way to rule out all competing variables. With many of my prayers, I really can't.

But there are some prayers where it might be possible to evaluate a direct link between prayer and the desired result. Nowhere is this more evident than in the prayer for healing. When I was on the faculty at Oral Roberts University, I vividly remember the first time I met Oral Roberts. Fresh from 6 years of teaching at South Dakota State University and a PhD in my hand, I accepted a teaching position at ORU and had dinner with Roberts. I felt like I was becoming a part of a wonderful expression of the healing ministry of Roberts. At that time, he was probably the leading "faith healer" in the world. What a great place to be employed! I could live out both my academic education as well as my spiritual beliefs. Utopia!

With great anticipation, I began not only to teach classes, but routinely participated in the Partner Meetings (partners were those who supported Oral Roberts) on campus, especially ushering at the Sunday morning healing service. Over the years at ORU I advanced from a faculty member to a department chairman and finally a dean. During that time I observed Roberts praying for the healing of tens of thousands of individuals.

Unfortunately, the longer I was at ORU witnessing how Roberts became a wealthy man from the gifts of his partners and seeing some of his partners give almost everything they had in hopes of receiving healing and/or wealth, my idealism gradually diminished, and I left ORU after 14 years disappointed and disillusioned. I don't know if I ever saw a healing; and I never saw a paraplegic, a quadriplegic, a person with cerebral palsy, muscular dystrophy, or individuals with other significant organic diseases healed. Many times I heard him say "God spoke to me and told me…" to do this or that. I also heard many of the evangelists and preachers that would come to ORU also tell us of the special messages they had received from God. They would give accounts of glorious healings in other places, usually in third world countries. I always wondered, why we didn't actually see the healings ourselves.

As much as I would like to report that many were healed at ORU, I never saw a single person with the above four diseases/disabilities healed. I saw great trust and faith, great belief, and then often great despair. Then came the rationalizations, which were many: 1) sometimes God heals over time; 2) sometime he heals in the resurrection; 3) always trust God since he knows best; 4) never question God; 5) perhaps there is some hidden sin or unbelief and that's why there was no healing; 6) some say these particular promises were only for the people of the time of Jesus and don't apply to today; and 7) maybe through this health problem God is working in the person. In any event, excuses were made as to why the promises found in the Bible didn't work. While at ORU, I attended a charismatic/evangelical mega-church in Tulsa. It taught the literal acceptance of the scripture and if the promises don't work for you, you need to examine your life. An example of this belief run amok was observed when a young couple who were very good friends of ours lost their baby to Sudden Infant Death Syndrome (SIDS). The counseling they received from the pastors of the church was that they needed to examine their lives to find the sin that must be present.

The bottom line is, if we are to take the scriptures literally, there are promises that our prayers will be answered. "Every promise in the book is mine." You can get all things if you believe according to the Bible. "All things for which you pray and ask, believe that you have received them, and they shall be granted you." (Mark 11:24, NAS) "Whatever you ask in my name, that will I do." (John 14:13,

NAS) "If you ask me anything in my name, I will do it." (John 14:14, NAS) "If you have faith as a mustard seed, you shall say to this mountain, 'move from here to there' and it will move. Nothing will be impossible for you." (Matthew 17:20, NAS) "If two of you agree on earth about anything that they may ask, it shall be done for them by my father." (Matthew 18:19, NAS) "Everything you ask in prayer, believing, you shall receive." (Matthew 21:22, NAS) "And if we know that he hears us in whatever we ask, we know that we have the requests which we have asked from him." (I John 5:15, NAS) "Be it done to you according to your faith." (Matthew 6:29, NAS)

You will be saved from all your troubles and protected from danger. "The righteous cry out, and the Lord hears them; he delivers them from all their troubles." (Psalms 34:17) "A thousand may fall at your side, 10 thousand at your right hand, but it will not come near you...no harm shall befall you...he will command his angels concerning you to guard you in all your ways." (Psalms 91:7-11) But does history and experience support that these promises will be fulfilled? I think not. Christians are not delivered from "all their troubles," sometimes children do go "begging" for bread, and we have seen disasters "come near your tent." If one is a literalist, how does one explain that these promises can't be counted on?

So, I speculate. How can one Christian claim God's protection for there being no damage to their home in a tornado when their Christian neighbor's home was destroyed? Did God choose to protect one person and not another? Did one trust more that the other?

These promises (and many more found in the Bible) are wonderful and speak to us of a God who personally cares about us. But it does not take much observation to determine that "every promise" doesn't come true. Can we count on them? Are they dependable? Maybe they are not to be taken literally. But if you're a literalist, do you just explain away these promises? Maybe blame the person for not having enough faith?

It is interesting that some people are more willing to put faith in the promises and prayer than in objective scientific evidence. The scientific method of discovery requires an observation and minimal threshold that some event will occur at least 95% of the time before it is concluded that this event is predictably true. What if we were to place that standard for fulfillment of the promises described in the Bible?

When I was at ORU, I initially believed strongly in the effectiveness of prayer. So, I proposed a study where we would document every person who went through the Oral Roberts prayer lines where Roberts prayed for them. Then we'd follow-up with everyone. Unfortunately, my request was turned down. In time I came to understand why. The leadership in the Oral Roberts ministry did not want to document the effectiveness of the prayers for healing. Rather, they would rely on the testimonies of the prayers that seemed to work as reported so they could write the story to make it sound pretty good. Of the thousands that were prayed for in any given time period, perhaps 10 testimonies may be reported—a far cry from the 95% statistical standard that is held out for science. What is also important to remember in regard to testimonies is the role faith and language has in them. If you are a believer in God's role as well as one's own faith in healing, then the admonitions in Romans 10:9-10, I Peter 2:24, and James 5:15-16 are very important to be followed. I well remember a young man at Oral Roberts University suffering from Cerebral Palsy. After being prayed for, he threw away his crutches and confessed publically that he was healed. For many days he struggled to walk around campus, often falling and significantly bruising himself. Finally, injured and defeated, feeling a failure for a lack of faith and what must have been an improper confession of his healing, he bandaged up his bruises and began using his crutches again. I only wish he was the only one I observed who followed this same pattern.

I remember as a child going to the healing services of William Branham in Chicago. It appeared that many were healed. I also remember vividly that my brother, who had lost an eye in an accident, was never one of those healed, and I always wondered why. Did God selectively decide who he would heal and who would not be healed? How did God decide that? Maybe these promises didn't apply to everyone. Maybe my family didn't have enough faith. Maybe our family had hidden sin; hence my brother was not healed. As a child, this was troubling to me.

As a college student during the Vietnam war, I knew of friends who prayed earnestly for family members to not get drafted and sent to Vietnam only to have them be drafted, sent to Vietnam, and get killed. My freshmen roommate was drafted into the Vietnam War and killed. I began to wonder if prayer really works. Perhaps the God "up there" and/or "out there" was not really out or up there. Maybe God does not intervene.

The greatest disappointment relative to Biblical promises and prayer was the lack of effectiveness as it related to the health and well being of my mother. Mom had a wonderful, total faith in God and in the literal interpretation of the Bible. If anyone was a "saint" on earth, it was my mother. Yet during her lifetime she suffered from various ailments and difficulties. In her youth she was abused by an alcoholic father. She was kicked out of her home as a teenager. From age 20 to well into her 40's she suffered from migraine headaches and severe back aches. In her 60's and beyond, she suffered from gastrointestinal reflux disease, numerous urinary tract infections, and then suffered a debilitating stroke, a broken hip, and dementia. All this time she prayed for relief, but none came until death. If the scriptures are to be taken literally, if anyone should have been healed, it was my mother. Did God withhold his healing and protection from her? I have difficulty accepting that. Was God teaching Mom, Dad, or others from Mom's suffering? I have difficulty accepting that as well. My childhood view of the Bible's promises has been greatly challenged by my observations of so many incidents when those promises didn't work. I have heard numerous rationalizations relative to Mom's situation; however, while they may make us feel better, they don't really address the issue. Maybe these wonderful promises are not meant to be taken literally. Maybe the song we sang in our childhood and youth of "every promise in the book is mine, every chapter, every verse, every line" is bad theology.

According to Mark, just before Jesus ascended into heaven, he told the 11 to "go into all the world and preach the good news to all creation. Whoever believes and is baptized will be saved...and these signs will accompany those who believe: In my name they will drive out demons; they will speak in new tongues; they will pick up snakes with their hands; and when they drink deadly poison, it will not hurt them at all; they will place their hands on sick people, and they will get well." (16:15-18) A wonderful promise! The question is, "is this true? Do these signs follow those who believe?" And, if we don't observe these signs following believers, what about the truth of the first statement where we can't observe the validity of it, that is, "whoever believes and is baptized will be saved." If the latter is not true, how do we know that the former is true? Maybe it's not. Maybe it is a childish belief that needs to be left behind.

As a child, I would sometimes ask about the many promises that did not seem to happen. Were these promises wishful thinking, similar to believing in Santa and the Tooth Fairy? My parents and religious figures who I knew would often become defensive and would tell me that we should never question the "Word of God." They warned us to not ask those questions because it would lead us to hell.

When I was a child, that answer seemed all right. It is a lot easier to just believe something, to have a "simple" faith, or ignore it when it does not seem right, rather than to question it and carefully examine it. In my early adult years, while I was busy raising a family and working, that answer also seemed all right. I didn't want to deal with it. Over the past 20 years, however, I have no longer been able to "just believe" or "ignore" statements of promise that just don't happen. Fulfilled promises appear to be the exception rather than the rule. It has been extremely difficult to change my view of the Bible that I have read and studied since my childhood. How can I deny authenticity of the scriptures? After all, aren't they the "Word of God"? Must I accept the truth of all the scriptures when the evidence is lacking and actually contrary? Perhaps God, not the God as described in the Bible, but the "God beyond God" as described by theologian Paul Tillich is "speaking" to me to grow up and leave behind my childhood faith.

In April of 2012, two teenagers died in separate events when parents chose prayer, believing in the literalness of the promises for healing in the Bible, and refused to provide medical care for treatable illnesses. (McCowan, Accessed June 2, 2012) and (Piatt, Accessed June 2, 2012) As has been my observations throughout this book, when the Bible is taken as the literal, written Word of God, serious negative consequences all too often occur. Too many innocent persons are hurt.

After receiving training at a bible training center in Tulsa, OK, Brian Baker returned to Australia and began a charismatic ministry that by 1989 was one of the largest in his country. In time he came to doubt his beliefs when he saw so many of the promises didn't happen. He admits, however, that it was not easy. "To consider an investigation or examination of my faith…was unthinkable. I had been fully indoctrinated to believe and had accepted that the Christian message…were absolute truths." (Introduction) In time he left his church, left preaching, and gave up his beliefs and Christianity altogether. He describes how his leaving Christianity was a gradual process over several years. Finally, he came to believe the Bible as the Word of God to be "nonsense." His story is not unique. In my studies I have come across many similar stories.

All scripture is God-breathed and is useful for teaching, rebuking, correcting and training in righteousness.

(II Timothy 3:16)

Chapter Ten

SELECTED TEACHINGS/STORIES AND THE CONCEPT OF INERRANCY

If a child disobeys, strikes or curses parents, he/she is to be executed. (Exodus 21:15, 17) Is this really what the God of Jesus would teach? Is this "God-breathed" and therefore, to be taken literally? If so, my parents should have put me to death long ago. In fact, if we are to take this literally, probably few children would survive childhood!!

The God of the Old Testament apparently does not like any person that has any type of physical problem. Anyone with a disability (blind, lame, mutilated faces, itching diseases, scabs, crushed testicles) cannot become a priest. (Leviticus 21:17-21) This can't be the teachings of the God of Jesus since he reached out to all those with diseases.

In Leviticus 19 there are many laws listed. A few we are familiar with and we readily accept such as: "Do not steal. Do not lie. Do not deceive one another." (vs 11). But there are also laws that are more challenging to accept such as: "Do not mate different kinds of animals. Do not plant your field with two kinds of seed. Do not wear clothing woven of two kinds of material." (vs 19) This last decree can also be found in Deuteronomy 22:11 "Do not wear clothes of wool and linen woven together." Additionally, in Leviticus 19:27 it states: "Do not cut the hair at the sides of your head or clip off the edges of your beard." Even evangelical/conservative Christians do not feel compelled to follow these laws. But, how do they rationalize accepting some of the laws and not others? Do evangelicals claim the entire Bible is to be taken literally but then rationalize the acceptance of some scripture as literal and others as not? Who decides?

And why do Christians eat pork when the Bible clearly forbids it? Deuteronomy 14:7-8 "you may not eat...the pig."

My early memory of the teachings of my Pentecostal church relative to the "Baptism in the Holy Spirit" was that after you accept Christ as your Lord and Savior, there was another experience that you should seek; the "Baptism in the Holy Spirit." I was taught, as is recorded in the book of Acts, proof of this experience is the "speaking in tongues." Of course, there were many Christians who did not believe in this experience such as Lutherans, Methodists, Baptists, and a multitude of other denominations. However, this was no consolation since we doubted whether most of them were Christians going to heaven anyway. I remember as a teenager praying, seeking, crying, and begging God to fill me with the Holy Spirit. Despite my sincerity, I did not at that time ever speak in tongues. So, I reasoned I was not good enough for God to fill me with his Holy Spirit. No matter how much I read the Bible, memorized scriptures, attended church Sunday mornings, Sunday evenings, Wednesday evenings every week, confessed my sins and sought God, it apparently was not good enough. I was a second class Christian since I didn't speak in tongues, prophecy, and interpret tongues. Or, sometimes I wondered, "Was this teaching valid or correct"?

At Oral Roberts University, students and faculty were required to attend a special class taught by Roberts called "Holy Spirit in the Now." He taught that we were filled with the Holy Spirit when we accepted Christ and that "speaking in tongues" or as he called it the "prayer language" was already within us and all we needed to do was release it. We should simply begin "babbling" and with practice we'd become comfortable with doing that and indeed that was "speaking in tongues." WOW!! That simple? It is not something God gives us, just something we do ourselves. So which doctrine was correct? The one my church originally taught me, the way that Oral Roberts explained it, or perhaps it was not a valid doctrine as was taught by many other churches?

Some evangelicals/churches will indicate that new revelation has "over turned" some of these verses, or that we are living in a new dispensation and under a new covenant. However, that leads to selective literalists who choose parts of the Bible that conform to their personal ideology and ignore the rest. Can you have it both ways, claim that the Bible is literally true in its totality and must be obeyed, and then claim that the Bible does not need to be totally obeyed?

The *New York Times* (Nov. 7, 2011) wrote a story about a book written by Michael Pearl, pastor of a conservative evangelical church in Pleasantville, TN. The book, *To Train up a Child* has sold more than 670,000 copies and is popular among Christian home-schoolers. In this book he advocates the systematic use of "the rod" to teach toddlers to submit to authority. The book says the Bible calls for corporal punishment and is supported by Biblical passages like, "He that spareth his rod hateth his son." He provides instructions for "switching" defiant children to provide "spiritual cleansing." Further instructions are given for using a switch for children from as early as 6 months old to discourage misbehavior. It describes how to make use of implements for hitting on the arms, legs, or back. Unfortunately, it has been reported that at least 6 deaths have been caused by parents using his book as a guide for raising their children. Again, when the Bible is taken literally and accepted as absolute truth, there is always a potential of causing damage.

The *Washington Post* (May 31, 2012) wrote about Mack Wolford, a pastor of a church in West Virginia who believed in the literal interpretation of the Bible. They followed the statements in Mark 16:17-18 that stated, "And these signs will follow those who believe, in my name...they will speak in tongues; they will pick up snakes with their hands; and when they drink deadly poison it will not hurt them at all." On a Sunday in May 2012 Mack did pick up a deadly snake that bit him. He refused medical attention and died late that night. He was 44. Mack's family has accepted his death as something that was ultimately God's will. The pastor laid down his life for his conviction, said his sister. Some of the people who attended his last Sunday service have struggled with Mack's death. "Sometimes, I feel like we're all guilty of negligent homicide," one man wrote in a Facebook message following Mack's death. "I went down there a 'believer.' That faith has seriously been called into question. I was face-to-face with him and watched him die a gruesome death…. Is this really what God wants?" It can be deadly to take the Bible literally and accepted as absolute truth.

In Genesis we read of the account of Noah and the flood (Genesis 6-7). All life on Earth was destroyed except Noah, his family, and a male and female of every living creature in an ark. Really? Is this the God of Jesus who would order such an event? Some who have calculated the size of such an ark and the flood have concluded this is not possible. My faith used to be blind enough to accept this event. I now doubt this story.

Genesis chapter 1 teaches us that the earth and the universe were created in 6 days about 6,000 years ago. I have heard too many pastors teach that this is to be accepted literally. Science has clearly refuted that claim with overwhelming evidence that the earth is billions of years old and we are still discovering how it came into being. It reminds me of the Middle Ages when individuals (like Galileo) were imprisoned because they did not accept the earth as the center of the universe. It is interesting to note, not only the Catholic Church held this position, but it was also supported by John Calvin and Martin Luther.

Saint Augustine wrote in the 4th century that "in matters that are so obscure and far beyond our vision, we find in Holy Scripture passages which can be interpreted in very different ways without prejudice to the faith we have received. In such cases, we should not rush in headlong and so firmly take our stand on one side that, if further progress in the search for truth justly undermines this position, we too fall with it." He went on to say that if Christians hold beliefs that are well known scientifically to be untrue, "it is disgraceful and dangerous thing for an infidel to hear a Christian, presumably giving the meaning of Holy Scripture, talking nonsense on these topics...for if they find a Christian mistaken in a field which they themselves know well and hear him maintaining his foolish opinions...how are they going to believe those books and matters that really matter?" (Taylor, p. 36-43)

Is it necessary for my faith in the God of Jesus to believe in the literalness of the story of creation, of the flood, and numerous other scriptures I have come to question? As I will discuss in later sections, thank God for the writings of Biblical scholars who have presented ample evidence that we can develop a "new" view of the Bible that allows one to "leave behind" much of our childhood faith and instead develop an "adult" faith.

Inerrancy of the Bible, the concept that the Bible is without error, is also a basic belief of most evangelical Christians. Let me provide just four examples of the many inconsistencies in the Bible. First, if we are to believe the Bible is without error and to be taken literally, I find that there are two different accounts of the last words of Jesus upon the cross. Luke 23:46 says "And when Jesus had cried with a loud voice, he said, Father, into thy hands I commend my spirit: and having said thus, he gave up the ghost." However, John 19:30 says "When Jesus therefore had received the vinegar, he said, 'It is finished' and he bowed his head, and gave up the ghost." Which of these two accounts is accurate? I know it is rather silly to even raise this question. However, if one is a literalist, how does one deal with the inconsistency? Often it is just ignored or some rationalization is given for the inconsistency.

Second, who was the father of Joseph? Was it Jacob or Heli? Matthew 1:16 says, "And Jacob begat Joseph the husband of Mary, of whom was born Jesus...." On the other hand, Luke 3:23 says "And Jesus...the son of Joseph, which was the son of Heli..." Which of these two accounts is the correct one?

Third, Matthew. 20:20-21 says "Then the mother of Zebedee's sons came to Jesus with her sons and, kneeling down, asked a favor of him. 'What is it you want?' he asked. She said, 'Grant that one of these two sons of mine may sit at your right and the other at your left in your kingdom.'" However, Mark records that it was not the mother who made the request to Jesus. Mark 10:35-37 says "Then James and John, the sons of Zebedee, came to him. 'Teacher,' they said, 'we want you to do for us whatever we ask.' 'What do you want me to do for you?' he asked. They replied, 'Let one of us sit at your right and the other at your left in your glory.'" So which account is accurate? Was it the mother or the two sons who made the request? Again, I know...it is rather trivial to even raise this question. However, if one is a literalist, how does one deal with the inconsistency?

Fourth, when Ahaziah, son of Athaliah began his reign, 2 Chronicles 22:2 says he was 42 years old. But, 2 Kings 8:26 says he was 22. One of these scriptures must be wrong. Michal, daughter of Saul, is said to have no children when she died. (2 Samuel 6:23) However, 2 Samuel 21:8 said she had five sons. Which is correct?

I realize that this could be dubbed as "nitpicking." However, if one believes the bible is "inerrant," how does one rationalize its errors and inconsistencies? In my discussions with those who believe the Bible is the inerrant Word of God, I find questions such as these to be either ignored or answered with some lame justification. Most don't want to deal with anything that challenges their beliefs. The more their belief system is challenged, the more vehemently they become in their attacks on the person raising the questions.

Count your blessings, name them one by one. Count your many blessings see what God has done

—Words from a hymn

Chapter Eleven

GOD'S BLESSINGS, GOD'S WILL, AND A PERSONAL GOD

In the Christian home and church where I spent my child and young adulthood, we believed that God was in charge of everything and we didn't really need to do much about it other than to pray and listen to God. He has your job, your partner, and everything lined up for you. (I am reminded of the new website, "Christianmingle.com" that advertises "find God's match for you." They report to have over 9 million subscribers as of April 2013.) Every hair on our head is numbered. God will personally take care of you. If everything goes well, you are blessed. You really didn't have anything to do with it. If a storm comes your way and all the homes around you are damaged and yours is not, it is because God blessed you. You are special.

A core problem in our country is the belief in and practice of radical individualism that not only is American as apple pie, but has infiltrated evangelical Christianity. Marcus Borg writes that we are probably the most individualistic culture in human history. As I reflect on my years at ORU and time as an active member of a large charismatic Tulsa church, I bought into the theology of prosperity, healing, and "name-it-and-claim-it"—give to God and God will give to you, or the popular "me-ism." It seems to me this is another way of saying individualism. I rarely heard messages on taking care of my neighbor since the focus was on the personal blessings for the believer. It was a message that fit in well with American individualism. After 14 years in this environment, seeing the abuses and the pain that such a theology caused in "partners" of Roberts as well as in the lives of students and faculty, I resigned in 1988, went to another university to teach, and stepped back and evaluated those 14 years in an objective setting. That began my journey to a new "adult faith."

Since leaving ORU, I have come to seriously question that theology and wonder if it is heresy. While you can find some scripture to support such beliefs, the over-riding theme of the life and teachings of Jesus was his concern for the poor and the disenfranchised, the importance of forgiveness, turning the other cheek, caring for your neighbor, kindness, compassion, his rejection of riches, and his emphasis on putting the group ahead of personal ambitions. History has shown that those who promote individualism do not value and appreciate those who preach a social gospel of "being my brother's keeper" or "loving my neighbor." Jesus, Martin Luther King, and Gandhi were all killed because of the social gospel they preached. Today conservative Christianity is leading the fight against anyone with whom they don't agree and are unwilling to look for ways to find common goals and speak a common language of hope. As Armstrong points out in her best-selling book *The Battle for God*, the greatest danger to civilization is fundamentalism in Islam, Judaism, and yes, Christianity. I now wonder if the conservative Christianity that was "fundamental" to my core values for over 40 years is part of the problem in our American culture. It has been a very painful observation to make.

The "me-ism" of evangelical Christianity is further reinforced by the titles of some of Joel Osteen's more than 50 books and CD's listed on Amazon such as: *It's Your Time: Activate Your Faith, Achieve Your Dreams, and Increase in God's Favor* (2009); *Become a Better You: 7 Keys to Improving Your Life Every Day"* (2009); *"Your Best Life Now: 7 Steps to Living at Your Full Potential"* (2007); *Living The Joy Filled Life: Six Easy Steps To Living A Life Of Victory, Abundance And Blessing* (2005); *See Yourself Successful* (2004). His books are examples of the theology of "it's all about ME." Osteen never graduated from college and is now pastor of a church with over 30,000 attending Sunday services.

Recently, as I relaxed on the 5-hour flight from Washington, DC to Phoenix, I thought about the great thanksgiving week we had spent with our daughter, her husband, and their 4-year-old daughter. How blessed we are as a family. The move to a new townhouse for them went well; our son-in-law is enjoying his responsibilities in the Marines (he has safely returned from 4 deployments to Iraq); our daughter loves being a mom; and our granddaughter, well, what can one say about her...she's just great! I thought of the song I often sang in my childhood and youth, "count your blessings, name them one by one." Indeed, on a daily basis I am counting my blessings and am so very, very thankful. I often wonder why I am so blessed. As I observe the national and international scene, I find myself feeling guilty. There are so many people in such great need. It seems like these days I shed tears alternating between those of joy regarding my circumstances and those of sorrow for people in such dire situations.

"Count your blessings, name them one by one...count your many blessings see what God has done." Indeed, for most of my life I have thanked God for all my blessings. But, over the past 10 to 15 years I have begun to wonder if this is good theology. Why would God chose to have me born in the USA, the land of opportunity, and another child born into a dreadful place such as Rwanda or Afghanistan wracked by violence and instability? Why would God choose to have me born into a loving and supportive family and another child born to a heroine/cocaine addicted mother and be "messed up" before even being born with little hope for a future?

Every once in awhile you have an experience that especially awakens you to carefully examine your belief system. Have you ever used the phrase, "There, but for the grace of God, go I?" For example, if you see a drunk, or a drug addict, or a homeless person, you might say, "there, but for the grace of God, go I." Donna and I confess that we have made those statements, probably all too often. As individuals and as a family, we are so blessed and fortunate. We have been taught in our religion that we should be thankful to God for all of our blessings. And, indeed, I am extremely thankful. But, are we actually falling into the trap of pride thinking that God is especially choosing to bless us?

While in Oslo the summer of 2010, we observed a group of disabled young adults touring a museum. Donna's first thought was "there, but for the grace of God, go I." And almost immediately, an overwhelming sense of guilt welled up in her, and she went over and sat down on a bench and asked God's forgiveness for thinking that God had somehow showered her with grace not given to the disabled persons. For the next hour, we took a break from our "touring" and talked about the concept of God's blessings.

So, I wonder. While we would like to think that God has personally showered us with such wonderful blessings, how should we respond? Why should God bless us and withhold his blessings from another? Does a loving God really control events to help some and allow others to be injured? Or in examining this from a very personal family perspective, how can we claim God's blessings and protection while one of our nieces is suffering from tumors in her jaw? What about my brother losing an eye in an accident when he was a young child and never regaining his sight in that eye? How can I claim God's blessings and protection when in 1995, our daughter almost died and lost 75% of her small intestine and has to live daily with the negative effects of that loss for the rest of her life?

As previously mentioned, perhaps the greatest disappointment relative to the idea of "God's blessings," is related to the health and well-being of my mother. Mom had a wonderful faith in God and in the literal interpretation of the Bible. If anyone was a "saint" on earth, it was Mom. Yet in her life she suffered from various ailments and difficulties. Perhaps, God neither gives nor withholds blessings.

Maybe, rather than verbally expressing our thanksgiving to God for our blessings, our response to our blessings should be to demonstrate an attitude of gratefulness by being an imitator of Christ in our actions and love of neighbor, i.e. feeding the hungry, giving water to the thirsty, looking after the sick, taking in the stranger, clothing the poor, and visiting the prisoner.

Both Donna and I have been active exercisers since we were in our 20's. At five feet tall, Donna was 103 pounds when she graduated from high school. Throughout her life she continues to be around 103 and looks trim and fit. Women often tell her how "blessed" she is to have been able to keep her slim figure as she grew older. Donna often says little in response to these comments, but she knows better. For it was not a special "blessing" that she is fit and has maintained her weight. Beginning at age 25 she began to jog 10 to 15 miles per week. That distance increased to 20 miles in her 30's and she was jogging 25 to 30 miles per week in her 40's and 50's. From age 25 to 60, she has jogged over 45,000 miles and burned over 4,000,000 calories, which amounts to 1,143 pounds. While working, she would often get up at 5:30 AM and jog 5 miles before returning home for breakfast and arriving at work by 8 AM. Her weight is not the result of any special blessing but has been maintained by diligently following the well-known principles of science relative to diet and exercise.

Recently while attending a yoga class, the instructor said she wanted to share a special experience with the class. She shared how she was so blessed by God as indicated by her experiences of the past week. Her car broke down and needed to be towed. She shared how she was blessed in that she did not have to pay a tow truck to take the car to the garage for repairs, but rather, a friend had a pick-up truck and used a chain to pull her car to the garage. Then, she shared how God had another friend loan her a car for a week so she would have transportation. Finally, she shared that when she found out the repair for the car would be $700, an amount that she did not have, another friend gave her the money to pay for the car repairs. For all this, she gave thanks to such a wonderful God she served who provided all that for her.

My take on her situation is different. To give credit to God for providing her the assistance is to trivialize her friends who went out of their way to help her. It is to take credit away from her friends who were the ones who provided her the help and to give thanks to someone else. It is like telling her friends that they didn't deserve the credit for helping her; it was really God. People often will say that God uses people to accomplish his work. Are they saying that the people would not do it themselves, but that God "pushed" them into doing his work? Are we not really free moral agents? Or, does God pull the strings, and we do this or that at his direction, often unknown to us?

My father and mother lived a life in complete faith that God would take care of them. At least that was their belief and their confessions. However, their lifestyle did not indicate that was always true. First of all, when Dad went to Montevideo, Minnesota in 1956 to begin a new church, he did not idly sit by and wait for God to supply his needs. No, he built a home with the help of many volunteers from the church. Then, with the knowledge, skill, and contacts he gained from the first home, he built a second home and sold it. He then continued to build homes "on the side" over the next 11 years while he also built a flourishing church. He had 2 full-time jobs! After 11 years, he was able to leave that church, sell a home, and had money in his pocket. Blessed by God? Or, blessed by his own hard work? I'd say the latter. I watched my dad work extremely hard to provide for his family. I admired that.

I wonder if on some level Karl Marx was correct when he wrote "religion is the opium of the people." He indicated that perhaps religion's purpose is to create illusory fantasies for individuals in their times of struggle. Religion gives a person, Marx said, hope and comfort just like a drug. Maybe that is the primary function of religion.

On September 11, 2001, only 20 people who were still inside the Twin Towers when they collapsed made it out alive, including 6 New York City firefighters from Ladder Company 6 in the city's Chinatown section. Capt. Jay Jonas was one of them. When people tell him that he was blessed by God that day, he refuses to accept that he was blessed saying, "that means 3000 others weren't and died. Does that mean they were not blessed by God that day? I think not." He flatly rejects that idea. So do I. I have come to believe that the theology of a personal God who has my life planned out, intervenes on my behalf from time to time, and blesses me are elements of my childhood, beliefs that need to be left behind.

Pearson makes an interesting observation relative to the concept of being thankful. "We are expected to present our meager thanks to God for any little blessing he bestows upon us, his cowering little servants. This is nothing more than a continuation of the toxic dynamic that is diminishing and destroying our world: God as master and believers are slaves. Rather, I think to be thankful is to recognize that everything, every experience and circumstance is interrelated, interconnected. To thank is simply to think and be conscious of the benefits and blessings of 'being.'" (p.189)

I like your Christ. I do not like your Christians. Your Christians are so unlike your Christ.

—Mohandas Gandhi

Chapter Twelve

RALPH REED & MIKE HUCABEE
IN OUR HOME

While at Oral Roberts University, I increasingly became involved in conservative politics. We had just come out of the 1960's-70's liberal rebellion against the "establishment" with "free love," the "drug" movement, Roe vs. Wade, and the coming out of gays and lesbians. For Christian conservatives, it seemed as if our county was on a path of moral destruction. Were not these the central issues that were leading our nation to annihilation? At that time I had a limited view of politics, a fundamentalist view of Christianity and the Bible, and it seemed as if the Democratic Party was contributing to our destruction and the Republican Party was more the party of moral decency.

While at ORU, we became acquainted with and hosted coffees in our home for conservative Republicans, including Jim Inhofe and Frank Keating when they ran for congress. While at that time both were defeated, in later elections Inhofe became a Republican senator from Oklahoma and Keating became a Republican governor of Oklahoma.

While I had great doubts about end-times theology and the ORU theology of healing and prosperity, I was still not ready to totally let go of my evangelical roots. They were still very strong. When we left ORU and moved to Jonesboro, Arkansas in 1988, and I started a new job at Arkansas State University (ASU), my activity in Christian/conservative politics expanded. I hosted a visit and a series of presentations by David Barton, Founder and President of WallBuilders (an ORU graduate) who gave convincing arguments on "America's Godly Heritage." I became a board member of the local Christian

Coalition group and gave presentations at Christian Coalition events. In 1992 we hosted a major meeting in Jonesboro. Ralph Reed, the national President of Christian Coalition was the keynote speaker. He also spent the night in our home and we visited extensively.

As part of Reed's visit to Jonesboro, we hosted in our home, Mike Huckabee (who later ran for the Republican nominee for President in the 2008 Republican primaries). In 1992 Huckabee had just re-signed as a Baptist pastor and was running for the senate from Arkansas. Reed was there to give Huckabee advice on how to run his senatorial campaign. For more than 4 hours we were part of a discussion and listened to Reed. Reed stated that to get the conservative Christian vote and be elected, Huckabee had to have two major strategies: 1) Share his "born again" Christian faith, his opposition to abortion and gay rights, and his support for prayer in schools; and very importantly, 2) Talk about his opponent's "anti-Christian values," how his opponent was too much of a socialist, that his election would lead to the weakening of our nation, and he needed to paint government as evil. The entire focus was on how to "smear" the opponent, how to "distort" his record, and how to make the opponent look like "Satan" in order to appeal to the conservative, church-going voters. The critical message that Reed gave was that once you convince the conservative Christians how ungodly your opponent is, they will support you no matter what your position is on other key issues. He painted conservative Christians as being somewhat ignorant and unconcerned about issues other than the moral issues as presented in the Bible.

I found the last part of Reed's comments extremely disturbing, i.e. conservative Christians were generally ignorant and/or did not care about issues other than social issues. In the discussion, Reed went on to indicate the positions Huckabee should support in order to get elected which included: the rights of individuals to own and carry guns; be against the socialist healthcare reform plan promoted by Clinton and the Democrats; be for a large military budget; support a reduction in taxes, especially for the high-end earners; support policies for children leaving public schools and going to private and charter schools; and support a reduction in entitlements especially for, as I understood what he was saying, the "least of these among us."

I was troubled by the advice Reed was giving Huckabee. I thought this was a "Christian" Coalition. Is "bashing" the opponent the only way we can get our person elected? Is that what Jesus would have us do? Don't the issues matter? Why the need to lie about the opponent? I happened to know that the man that Huckabee was running against was a fine Christian, had a solid family, and was honest and ethical. But to elect Mike Huckabee, those things did not matter. The message must include a constant attack of the opponent. And to get the Christian vote was to focus only on the moral issues.

But, I did care about more issues than just the narrow "moral" issues. I wondered, "Aren't there additional issues that should matter to Christians?" What policies would Jesus endorse? Is it really Christian to own and carry guns? Is it Christian to push for lower taxes, reduce government, and have a large part of the government budget go to the military? Is it really Christian to deny healthcare for the poor? Is unregulated capitalism a Christian value? What about Christ's command to feed the hungry, clothe the naked, take care of the widows and orphans, love your enemies, do good to those who abuse you, and visit those in prison? Shouldn't the Christian Coalition be supporting policies that accomplish those goals? Clearly, these issues were not important to them!

One key item in this discussion was healthcare. Since I was in the health promotion field and had studied and seen the significant need for healthcare reform, I had come to believe that Jesus would want to support a healthcare program that made sure the "least of these among us" would be provided healthcare. So, I was troubled that Reed indicated Christians were to oppose healthcare reform. That did not seem Christian to me.

At the conclusion of that evening in 1992, I was very disappointed. Clearly, I was naive to have thought that if the "Christian Coalition" were "Christian", it would seek to follow the teachings of Jesus. It would have positions on the care for the poor and the "least of these among us." I saw an unholy alliance forming between political conservatives and conservative Christians. The political conservatives were exploiting the passion and narrowness of the conservative Christians to get them to vote for their agenda. My response was to drop my membership in Christian Coalition and the Republican Party, registered as an Independent, and I took a 10-year sabbatical from political activity; using this time to read extensively about the teachings of Jesus and how these teachings should guide my life, my thoughts, and my political philosophy. Writers, such as Jim Wallis of Sojourners, have significantly influenced my thinking as well as Richard Fox, *Reinhold Niebuhr: A Biography.* (1985); Robert Jensen, *All my Bones Shake: Seeking a Progressive Path to the Prophetic Voice* (2009); Robin Meyers, *Saving Jesus from the Church* (2009); Marcus Borg, *The Heart of Christianity: Rediscovering a Life of Faith* (2003); and Philip Yancey, *Soul Survivor: How my Faith Survived the Church* (2001), to mention just a few. (See Sources and Resources at the end for a more complete list of books that have had an influence on my thinking the past 20 years.) These in-depth readings have changed my life, my way of thinking and my beliefs. Not only did I revise my political views, but also my theological and spiritual understandings.

I now strive to support policies that I believe represent the teachings and life of Christ relative to feeding the hungry, providing for the homeless, clothing the naked, taking care of the widows and orphans, providing healing healthcare for everyone, loving your enemies, doing good to those who abuse you, visiting those in prison, making sure we do not neglect the young, old, and disabled, and providing educational opportunities for everyone. I am against policies that favor the wealthy over the middle class and the poor and seek to deny freedom for the oppressed. *In American Fascists: The Christian Right and the War on America*, Hedges paints an ugly picture of how the religious right is plotting to destroy America as we know it today and turn it into a "Christian" empire. I wish I could say he's got it wrong, but my experience and evidence indicate he is on target.

It is interesting to note that Ralph Reed went on to become a key advisor to President Bush and Bush's approach to the 2000 and 2004 elections was exactly as Reed had advised Huckabee: attack your opponents, spread falsehoods, and above all, demonize all who disagree with you. You see that happening again relative to Obama as the right attacks him with a vengeance. What is most disheartening is those attacks are often led and supported by "Christians." I can understand when Rush Limbaugh attacks, but when Christian organizations are just as hateful, they don't speak for me or represent the Christ I serve.

Keating (Accessed October 21, 2009) reports that Richard Land, president of the Southern Baptist Ethics and Religious Liberty Commission, the public-policy arm of the largest Protestant denomination in the United States, said this about the Obama administration: "I want to put it to you bluntly. What they are attempting to do in healthcare, particularly in treating the elderly, is not something unlike what the Nazis did. It is precisely what the Nazis did." He stated that he was giving "the Dr. Josef Mengele Award" to White House adviser Ezekiel Emanuel. Mengele was a Nazi doctor who conducted cruel experiments at the Auschwitz death camp during the Holocaust. I don't believe such attacks represent the teachings of Jesus.

In a revival type speech, in March of 2012 Greenwell Springs

Baptist Church pastor Rev. Dennis Terry introduced 2012 Republican Presidential candidate Rick Santorum to his congregation in Baton Rouge, Louisiana. "I don't care what the naysayers say; this nation was founded as a Christian nation.... There is only one God and his name is Jesus. I'm tired of people telling me that I can't say those words.... Listen to me. If you don't love America, if you don't like the way we do things, I have one thing to say—GET OUT. We don't worship Buddha, we don't worship Mohammad, we don't worship Allah, we worship God, we worship God's son Jesus Christ." Christians, according to Rev. Terry, are the conscience of the state and even the key to turning the economy around. The pastor offered some pointed words about abortion, gay marriage, and prayer in schools, shouting about 'sexual perversion' and putting God back in Washington, D.C. (*Huffington Post Video*, Accessed March 19, 2012) Again, I don't believe Jesus would endorse such attacks.

The conservative right continues to attempt to frame almost every issue whenever they can as an attempt by the Democrats to take away religious liberty and/or the Democrats not being Christian. Note all the efforts to demonize Obama over his religion and even his being born in America. It is consistent with the advice Reed gave to Huckabee in 1992 in our home in Jonesboro, Arkansas. I shall never forget it. I have often felt like Anne Rice, whose novels including, *Christ the Lord: Out of Egypt* and *Christ the Lord: The Road to Cana* have sold over 100 million copies. The *USA Today* reported on July 20, 2010, that she was fed up with the followers of Christ. She posted on her Facebook page, "For those who care, and I understand if you don't: Today I quit being a Christian. I'm out. I remain committed to Christ as always but not to being 'Christian' or to being part of Christianity. It's simply impossible for me to 'belong' to this quarrelsome, hostile, disputatious, and deservedly infamous group. For 10 years, I've tried. I've failed. I'm an outsider. My conscience will allow nothing else...

In the name of Christ, I refuse to be anti-gay. I refuse to be anti-feminist. I refuse to be anti-artificial birth control...In the name of... Christ, I quit Christianity and being Christian. Amen."

Another political/moral issue that has been an extremely difficult issue for me is abortion. Prior to Roe v Wade, I never thought about it. In the 1970's when abortion became legal, the religious right made an issue of it, equated it with murder. Since I was on the religious right side of the fence at that time, I accepted the evils of abortion. It is often easy to be against something that does not affect you. It is easy to not give serious thought to very difficult issues.

Then everything changed for me in May of 1995. Our married daughter almost died of a blood clot in her small intestine. After 3 weeks in the hospital, 2 weeks of which she has no memory, and an operation to remove 75% of her small intestine, she went home to recover. Soon thereafter, her physician told her that for her to become pregnant would be very dangerous for both her and the baby. One or both of them could die. All of a sudden, the danger and the fear of her becoming pregnant became very real. It did not take Donna and me very long to modify our previously held position on the evils of abortions. If our daughter ever accidently became pregnant, we'd fully support her having an abortion to make sure her life was saved. Of course, abortion is a sad and tragic procedure. However, it must remain legal, and the decision must remain between the woman and her doctor.

My pro-choice belief was further reinforced by the work of some of my colleagues with drug addicts in a health promotion project in the 1990's. Our research team came in contact with drug addicts giving birth to babies who, because of their mother's drug habits, were born with numerous health problems, many of which would destine the child to a life of misery, addiction, and often disabilities. Our entire team came to support the need for abortions to be legal and available. For a baby to thrive and develop requires a mother who loves and is capable of raising a child. No child should be forced to be born to a mother who is not able or willing to provide all the love and attention the child needs.

My wife's work at a health clinic in Flagstaff and our daughter's experience as a nurse in labor and delivery at a hospital in Southern California further reinforced my view. Both of them experienced mothers giving birth to babies who were destined to a life of poverty and numerous other health problems. We all became advocates of the "morning after pill." Yes, abortion should be the last resort, but it needs to be kept legal. The church needs to better understand the needs of women and be compassionate on this very difficult issue. To force a woman to carry an unwanted fetus is cruel for both the mother and the child.

Since I have primarily been a part of the evangelical/fundamental wing of the Christian Church, I assumed that most, if not all, of the Christian Churches would have positions being totally opposed to abortion. To check out that assumption, I went to the Pew Forum on Religion and Public Life (http://pewforum.org/docs/?DocID=351) where they summarize official positions on abortion by various religious groups. I find that indeed, Christian denominations have varying positions on abortion. I also found it interesting that a number of religions other than Christianity have diverse positions on abortion. Many place the value of the woman ahead of the fetus as is the Jewish position on abortion that states: "…the fetus is not a person, it has no rights." The decision should be left to the woman, her doctor, and her rabbi. The Bibles clear answer is that life begins with the first breath. Abortions occurred during the time of Jesus, and there are no pronouncements on abortion by Jesus.

It is revolting how the very complex and difficult issue of abortion has become a political wedge issue, just as Ralph Reed predicted in my living room in 1992. Rather than see it as a very troubling issue that women have to deal with, many make it an issue of "faith" and all too often do it with hypocrisy. Take Rick Santorum whose positions against abortion and his efforts to restrict and eliminate its legal status are very well known. He is against abortion even in the case of incest or rape. He supported a bill in congress, known as the Unborn Victim's of Violence Act of 2004, that would make abortion a crime if in causing harm to a pregnant women the unborn fetus is injured. (PoliGu.com. Accessed March 20, 2012)

What is less well known is the situation relative to the pregnancy of his wife. In October 1996, his wife Karen was in her 19th week of pregnancy, the second trimester. At a routine doctor's visit, they discovered the fetus had a significant problem and surgery was done in an attempt to repair the problem. Within a few days, Karen developed a life threatening infection and they were faced with the dreadful choice of taking antibiotics that might induce labor or risking that she would probably die. Since they had 3 children at home, they made the very difficult choice that the children needed their mother; therefore she took the medicine and a "miscarriage" happened. Gabriel Michael Santorum was born and died within 2 hours. (Miller. Accessed March 21, 2012)

Santorum argues vociferously that their actions did not constitute an abortion. While technically true, many would contend that given his absolute opposition to abortion, he is really "playing a word game." Some would claim the "miscarriage" was an "abortion." As Lisa Miller wrote, "Abortion is complicated...and private.... Abortion makes many Americans squeamish, but they want it to be legal...even those who think abortion should always be legal, also believe it's morally wrong. Real people understand that at any moment they, or someone they love, could find themselves in a situation [where they] don't want, can't afford, can't sustain, or can't nurture a child."

(Miller. Accessed March 21, 2012)

Caitlin Moran (2011), a British writer, devotes a chapter in her book to the issue of abortion. She discusses her own decision to have an abortion. Already having 2 children, she was convinced that she would not be able to do a good job raising the third child so that "by whatever rationale you use, ending a pregnancy is incalculably more moral than bringing an unwanted child into this world." (p. 271-72) "Not even for a second did I think I should have this baby. I had no dilemma, no terrible decision to make—because I knew, with calm certainty, that I didn't want another child now…I can honestly say that my abortion was one of the least difficult decisions of my life… . I knew that to commit my life to another person might very possibly stretch my abilities to the breaking point." She added, "Our view of motherhood is still so idealized…I am vexed with the idea that, by having an abortion, a woman is somehow being un-motherly—that the absolute essence of womanhood is to sustain life, at all costs." (p. 272-73) Being a woman, she adds, is far more than bringing children into the world.

A related issue that is being exploited and used as a wedge issue is contraception. It seems disingenuous to deny a woman contraception and also deny her the right to the morning after pill and/or an abortion. These positions advocated by conservative, evangelical Christians are hurtful and mean-spirited. In the life and teachings of Jesus, I see no indication that he would have supported such positions.

I understand the previous paragraphs have pointed out problems I see with conservative Republicans. My concern has been over the unholy alliance that has been formed between political conservatives and evangelical conservatives. Christians are being used by political and economic conservatives. Christians are voting against policies that Jesus taught us in the Bible.

Richard Stearns, President of World Vision, wrote in his excellent, moving, and challenging book, *The Hole in our Gospel*, "What is the Christian faith about...what does God expect of me?" (p.1) "One of the disturbing things about church history is the church's appalling track record of being on the wrong side of the great social issues of the day." (p. 190) Historically, the church was complicit in America's terrible treatment of Native Americans, in its support of slavery, and was generally against women's rights denouncing those who were supportive as "atheists, socialists, communists." (p. 191) Amazingly, these are many of the same tactics that are used today by the Religious Right. Stearns goes on to write, with Christianity's terrible track record, "what are the injustices in our world right now that we cannot see?" (p. 196) He states that in the last 30 years the word 'evangelical' has gone from an 85% favorable rating to only a 3% favorable rating by those with no strong religious background. He feels the cause is that evangelicals have joined the "cultural wars" and are no longer known for their concern for the "least of those among us" and are now known for the "wars" they are fighting and what they are against. They are not willing to "live peacefully with anyone who doesn't believe what they believe." (p. 227) "We have, in fact, reduced the gospel to a mere transaction involving the right beliefs." (p. 243) He calls for Christians to return to the mission that Jesus proclaimed and Stearns sees as the "hole in our Gospel" which is caring for the "least of these among us...the lepers, the poor, the sick, the oppressed." (p. 240) Perhaps Mohandas Gandhi said it best, "I like your Christ; I do not like your Christians. Your Christians are so unlike your Christ."

More Christians have left the church because of the Bible than for any other single reason

—Marcus Borg

Chapter Thirteen

CONCLUSIONS ON THE BIBLE AS THE WORD OF GOD

While there is much good advice and wisdom found in the Bible, as has been discussed throughout these pages, believing that the Bible is totally the literal and infallible Word of God can have significant destructive and detestable consequences. The history of mankind reveals the negative results of man accepting the Bible as the literal Word of God. From wars to discrimination practices to believing the earth is the center of the universe to decrying vaccinations, Bible believing persons have distorted the Word of God. Just take the beliefs about vaccinations. Silverman (November 2001) writes that Timothy Dwight, President of Yale University from 1795 to 1817 spoke against the new medical invention called vaccination. "If God had decreed from all eternity that a certain person should die of small-pox," he said, "it would be a frightful sin to avoid and annul that decree by the trick of vaccination." Vaccination and inoculation were condemned by Protestant and Catholic leaders alike. Edward Massey, an English theologian, published a thesis in 1772 on "The Dangerous and Sinful Practice of Inoculation." In Boston, clergymen and devout physicians formed an Anti-vaccination Society, declaring that "the law of God prohibits the practice." Some even proposed that those who gave inoculations should be tried for attempted murder.

I believe one cannot be honest with oneself and accept the Bible as the literal Word of God. How can a thinking person on this earth accept that a certain book written over 2000 years ago contains the words of some god who lives in the sky and demands absolute acceptance and obedience to its statements? Or as Wheaton College graduate and now professor at Norte Dame University, Smith (2011) says about accepting the Bible as the literal written Word of God, "[It is] an untenable position that ought to be abandoned in favor of a better approach...I think reason and evidence show it is impossible to defend...is misguided...it does not and cannot live up to its own claims." (p. vii-ix)

In an October 2012 poll conducted by the Pew Research Center (Pew Forum on Religion & Public Life. "'Nones' on the Rise" Accessed October 23, 2012) 32% of respondents under the age of 30 and 20% of all adults in the United States have no religious affiliation, up from 15% just 5 years ago. It has been suggested that a major contributing factor for the young questioning the existence of God, and many adults leaving the church, comes from popular Christianity seen on TV, heard on the radio, and emphasized in the media. Popular Christianity is predominately evangelical and sees the Bible as the inerrant Word of God. As Borg notes, many people leave the church over the literal interpretation of the Bible.

As I have discussed, I no longer view the Bible the same as most evangelicals do. In order for me to believe in the God of Jesus and to remain a Christian, I've chosen to "leave behind" my childhood view of the Bible and understand and accept the Bible as more progressive Christians do. I no longer see it as the literal, factual, infallible, and without error written Word of God. It is important to note that viewing the Bible as literal, factual, and absolute is actually a product of the last few centuries. Borg (*The Heart of Christianity*) writes that Biblical inerrancy and infallibility were first mentioned in the 17th century and the concept of literalism commences from the late 1800's. Yet, with all its flaws and problems, the Bible is central to the teachings of Christianity, forms an "anchor" for Christian faith, and is not to be ignored.

While we recognize the Bible as the foundation of our Christian faith, especially the teachings of Jesus, I wonder if the teachings of Marcion (A. D. 80-160) were not correct. He taught that the God of the Old Testament was so totally different from the God of Jesus that he rejected the God of the Old Testament altogether. He advocated that the Christian Bible should not include the Old Testament. If a text portrays Yahweh as acting violently, Marcion says it didn't actually happen. This view was ultimately rejected by the church and Marcion's teachings were declared heresy. However, support of Marcion's teaching at that time was widespread. More recently, Biblical scholar Eric Seibert (2009) attempted to reconcile the loving God of the New Testament and the harsh God of the Old Testament. His conclusions support that of Marcion in that the harsh God of the Old Testament doesn't exist. It is important in understanding the story of Marcion to acknowledge that the books of the Bible were selected and voted on by church (political) leaders of the day—very fallible men. Perhaps if the early church leaders had accepted the teachings of Marcion, Christianity today would be significantly different. It is extremely important to note that there were many competing versions of Christianity in the early days of the church.

What is clear from my readings of Biblical scholars is that the emerging way of seeing the Bible is as a human product reflecting our spiritual ancestors' experiences of God, their stories about God, and how they viewed life with God. Borg indicates that the "emerging Christian paradigm" focuses on a historical-metaphysical reading of the Bible: historical in the sense of Biblical texts being read/interpreted in their historical context; metaphorical in the sense of not being dependent on factuality, but often yielding a "more-than-literal" meaning of the texts. In other words, some event may not have actually happened as recorded but we can gain much insight from that event. He further states that the Bible is sometimes mistaken; as I have described in considerable detail in the previous sections.

Meyers writes, "The Bible is not literally the Word of God but a collection of human words about God, inspired, but covered with human fingerprints. Taken out of context, scripture has been and continues to be used to defend the indefensible: slavery, anti-Semitism, and the degradation of women, minorities, and those outside the sexual, social, or economic mainstream. It has been used to smear science, to sanction war...to support the divine right of kings. As God has revealed new truth to each generation, the Bible has often been used to resist it, justify violence against its adherents, and divide creation into those who are saved by believing certain things and those who are lost and dispensable because they dared to question them. The very book that preserves the remarkable teachings of Jesus...is now the hammer of orthodoxy and thus betrays the spirit of the Galilean sage to whom it testifies." (p. 216) Additionally he writes, "The Bible is a 'library of books' a far-flung and diverse collection of literature that is neither infallible nor inerrant. It is entirely a human product. We have come to worship the Bible. It has become an idol for us. The same is true with Jesus. He came to point us to God, but within a couple centuries of his death, Jesus became a person to worship and the true Jesus is lost." (p. 29)

Pearson, a graduate of ORU who went on to found a large evangelical/charismatic church in Tulsa before leaving it for a more progressive view of the Bible and theology, writes "The Bible is not a Christian book...the Bible is a book of history and allegory. It is a book of myth, magic, and miracles that sheds light on our varying interpretations of God...I respect the Bible, but inspect it as well." (p. 119) He states, "One of the hallmarks of the limited mode of thought by which we define God...is an obsession with interpreting the words of our holy books or scripture to be absolute truth. Anytime that knowledge and a version of the truth are considered to be absolute, fundamentalism is the result; 'The Bible [God] says it, I believe it, that settles it' is closed-minded, willful ignorance, and is chilling for the future of our world." (p. 127)

Pearson continues that it makes little sense "that we are supposed to live by [the Bible] exclusively as inviolable writ" considering the Bible was "written by flawed men long after the fact, colored by prejudice and exaggeration." (p. 127) I am not denouncing the Bible, Pearson states, but "I don't view it as the inspired Word of God as much as the word of men about God, as they perceived God through their often jaded, human perspectives. I would like to see it read and placed in its proper, less idolatrous, place." (p. 128) Though he loves and lives by the scriptures and finds them a source of inspiration and learning to fuel his own growth, Pearson says "I no longer believe they are the inerrant sources of truth as I once did. I don't define God by them or confine God to them." (p. xxii)

John A. T. Robinson indicates that "the whole world-view of the Bible has changed.... In the last century a painful but decisive step forward was taken in recognition that the Bible does contain 'myth', and that this is an important form of religious truth." This understanding of the Bible has been gradually acknowledged by all theologians "except extreme fundamentalists." (p. 32-33)

Another theologian who has had a significant impact on my spiritual journey has been Bart Ehrman, because his early life was so much like mine. Since God was found in the Bible, that is, since the Bible is the written Word of God, he initially went to the fundamentalist Moody Bible Institute and studied Bible. He felt that to know God intimately, he needed to study and intimately know the Bible. Upon graduation from Moody, he went to Wheaton College to further study the Bible and literature. Again, his goal was to find God through the extensive study of the Bible, the inerrant, written Word of God to be accepted literally in its totality. From Wheaton, he went to Princeton where he earned his doctorate in New Testament where his focus was on Greek and Hebrew manuscripts. To know God he needed to find and read the original manuscripts of the Bible which he felt would contain the actual Words of God. Upon graduation from Princeton, he then began an academic and scholarly career as a university faculty member at the University of North Carolina. For the past 30 years he has been recognized as a scholar on the early foundations of Christianity. He says that as he examined historical documents, searched for the original writings of the Bible, and carefully studied the oldest documents available, with great disappointment he discovered the Bible to be a very human book and not the Word of God as he had believed since childhood. It significantly changed his belief system. As he states, "I did not change my mind willingly—I went down kicking and screaming…I resisted it with all my might…it became clear to me over a long period of time that my former views of the Bible as the inerrant revelation from God were flat-out wrong." (*Jesus Interrupted.* 2009, p. xi) What is interesting is that Ehrman states that for years the vast "majority of scholars teaching at universities and seminaries…do not believe in the inerrancy of the Bible." (p. 3) But, it is important to state, that these scholars "are not questioning God himself. They are questioning what the Bible has to say about God." (p.11)

Smith, also a Wheaton College graduate, has written a book, *The Bible Made Impossible,* where he presents compelling arguments why Christians should abandon the concept of Biblicism. Biblicism, he says is the idea that the Bible is exclusive in its authority, is infallible, self-sufficient, has internal consistency, is self-evident, and has universal application. He makes an interesting point that "more than a few faculty at different biblicist-oriented evangelical institutions actually personally do not subscribe to Biblical inerrancy and other elements of biblicism….yet will not 'come out of the closet' with those private disbeliefs for fear of losing their jobs and endangering their careers." (p. 183-184) At the 50th reunion of my high school graduation, I spoke to a classmate with whom I had not seen or spoken in 50 years. I knew he had entered the ministry so I sought him out to visit with him. He spoke of his recent retirement from the pulpit and felt for the first time he did not have to be the "defender of the faith" and could now speak honestly about his doubts of his Christian faith. He shared how he now met weekly for coffee with a group of other retired pastors who all felt greatly relieved that they could now be honest with themselves about reservations of their beliefs and what they had preached for many years. He spoke of the struggle that many pastors had that they could not be honest with their congregations since parishioners didn't ever want to hear any hint of doubt from their pastor.

In the first part of these writings, I constantly challenged the idea of "Did God really say that?" "Is this really God's word?" and "Does it make sense based on what we know today?" In summary of my reconstructed view of the Bible, in addition to the many authors I've read on the topic, I especially draw on the writings of noted Biblical historian Karen Armstrong (*A History of God.* 1993; *The Case for God.* 2009) and Paul Dorn ("*Really? Did God Say That*" and "*Did God Say That? Part 2.*" Accessed April 9 2012) who both express so well what I understand to be the most commonly accepted understanding of the Bible by Biblical scholars. I understand and accept today that the Bible was not written to us or for us, but within and for ancient communities. It is their stories, not God's infallible, inerrant, and absolute story. It was written by people over a period of hundreds of years to explain their interpretations of their life experiences. It is their understanding of how to live life with God based upon the knowledge and beliefs of their day.

For centuries, humans have considered the classic questions of life such as; how did all this begin; where did we come from; questions of suffering, evil, and what is our future. Lacking scientific knowledge, ancient beliefs included an understanding that the earth was flat and the sun, moon, and stars all rotated around the earth. It was thought that gods lived above the earth and sporadically came down to earth in nature or among people. The discipline of Theology was born. God talked to selected men and sent violent storms. What could not be understood was attributed to the gods, what scholars call "the god of the gaps."

Ancient tribes had their own god or gods who often were described as having the physical/emotional characteristics of humans. It was believed they were very powerful and could be manipulated by sacraments. They also could cause chaos if displeased by the actions of people. Additionally, the gods were believed to fight among themselves. So if one tribe conquered another, it was believed it was because that tribe's god was more powerful than the other tribe's god.

Johnson (1987) writes that the Jews are the only people "in the world today that possess a historical record...which allows them to trace their origins back into very remote times." Around 4000 years ago this specific tribe conquered most of the other tribes in the area. It was believed their god overcame the gods of the other tribes and gave them control over the land. Their god had ordered them to conquer other people without mercy and they were just following orders. Over a period from about 1000 BCE to about 200 CE, many of these traditional oral stories were written, and in time compiled into the Hebrew Bible, which was affirmed by them to be sacred.

In ancient days priests and prophets represented the gods. These men wielded a great deal of influence. In order to consolidate power it was necessary for rulers to collaborate with the priests and prophets to influence the beliefs of the day. It was eventually claimed that their god whom they called Yahweh, resided in Jerusalem and controlled affairs to the benefit of their own nation. In some ways, the overall story can be viewed as one of consolidation of political power through the use of religion and vice versa. Among the perceptions of the universe and the political stories are other writings that offer wisdom and advice for daily living as well as explanations of events that had occurred and warnings about consequences of ignoring the advice.

The Bible, a rich resource of ancient thoughts, inspires us to ask questions and discover our own stories and interpretations of life. We find many wise recommendations of how we should live our lives and relate to others. In the Bible we find Jesus challenging the religious and political systems of his day and his demonstration of unconditional acceptance and love. By studying the Bible in its historical context rather than literally, we are better prepared to interpret the stories for today. From the gospels, we understand the parables of Jesus as a teaching method (not necessarily facts) to reveal truths. Some of the stories are no doubt true and others probably not. Recognizing them as written during different political and religious times can assist us today as we ask; "Why was this gospel written when it was and what did it mean then?" "To whom was it written?" and, "What does this mean for us now?" Without understanding Biblical characters in their historical-metaphorical context, we risk making them say something that was not the original intent. What is most important is that we don't misuse the Bible; claim it to be the absolute, literal, inerrant Word of God; and use it to demand obedience to its pronouncements.

The Bible includes stories that provide interesting political and religious intrigue and are fascinating when read in the context of what was going on in the world where the stories originated. These stories can be especially instructive when read with an open mind unencumbered by presuppositions or religious dogmas, opinions, and creeds, and discussed in a conversation with other open-minded persons. By continuously seeking truth (not just answers), we contribute to the enhancement of political, religious, and social thought as we learn to live peacefully together in our universe and to be transformed (born again). As noted earlier, the Bible is central to the teachings of Christianity and forms an "anchor" for Christian faith. Christians should read, meditate, interact, and discuss its teachings on a regular basis, but don't follow it indiscriminately.

As I wrote in the Prologue, "these are my thoughts." They represent my opinion today. I expect they will continue to evolve as I study, reflect, engage in conversations, and have new experiences. As succinctly as I can, these are my conclusions today as I have reconsidered the Bible.

1. The Bible is not the written Word of God. It is a book written by humans, describing their interpretation of events, and their own personal beliefs and ideas.

2. The Bible is not to be taken literally. Rather, it is history, allegory, myth, and metaphor.

3. History has shown that taking the Bible literally has lead to slavery, discrimination, wars, denial and repression of scientific evidence, death, and a multitude of other evils.

4. The Bible is not inerrant. Rather, the Bible contains errors, contradictions, and recommendations and laws that modern cultures do not accept.

5. The Bible is a book written by many authors over an extended period of time. It was written for people of a different time, in a different place, with a limited view of the world.

6. The Bible was put together by a committee of persons often motivated by their own beliefs and political affiliations.

7. The Bible describes the life and teachings of Jesus written more than 30-70 years after his death. Read and study his life but do so understanding that the accuracy of events and his statements can be legitimately questioned.

Discovering Progressive Christianity

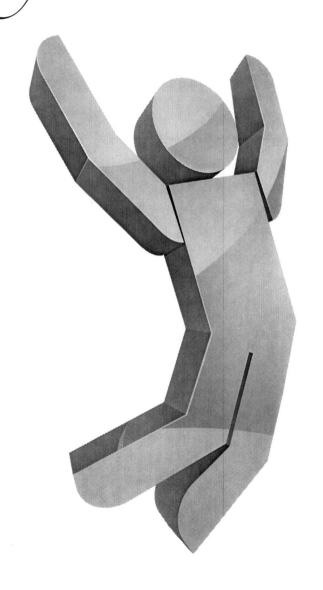

It is impossible to go back when you've outgrown who you were.

—Author unknown

Chapter Fourteen

AM I STILL A CHRISTIAN?

As my theology has progressed and I have "let go" of my belief in the Bible as the literal, inerrant Word of God, I've wondered what do I believe? What do I believe about God, Jesus, prayer, heaven, and other classic doctrines of the church? What is the authority for my faith? I am reminded of the statement by Michael Krasny, "I don't believe in God, but I miss him." (p. 3) He discusses his journey as a believing child to an agnostic adult. He wrote, "How can I make up for the loss of a God who once felt real, comforting, close and personal. How does one fill that vacuum?" (p. 5) To change one's life-long beliefs is one of the hardest things to do. How does one "let go" of the simplicity of a former belief system to a more complicated and mysterious faith with no formulas or supernatural interventions?

I believe what Krasny is saying is that he misses the "concept" of God. As children from evangelical families, we are brought up to believe that God watches over us, protects us, has the hairs on our heads numbered, and is a personal God. Many churches, pastors, and families proclaim this image of God. I remember how we taught our children that if you are nice, Santa will bring you gifts at Christmas. We did a good job instilling that image of Santa into our children and they genuinely believed in Santa. As they grew older and finally realized there was not a Santa, our son at about age 10, once told us, "I miss Santa. I miss looking forward to Christmas and the idea that Santa would come to our home and bring me gifts." And so it is, when we leave behind the Bible as the Word of God and the image of a personal God that the Bible creates, we miss that depiction of God. So I needed to fill the void with an image of God and view of the Bible that was satisfying and fulfilling but also authentic and honest. While this has been an agonizing task, it has also been extremely rewarding.

When I read Borg's book *The Heart of Christianity* in which he writes such a logical but painful deconstruction of my evangelical/fundamentalist views, I thought, "well then, how can Borg even be a Christian? How can I still be a Christian?" Then, with a great deal of insight and wisdom, he reconstructed his belief in his poignant section "Why be a Christian?" at the end of his book. This section outlines how I currently view being a Christian.

However, how important is it to be called a "Christian"? As mentioned earlier, I often feel like Ann Rice who, being fed up with the followers of Christ, posted on her Facebook page, "Today I quit being a Christian. I'm out. I remain committed to Christ as always but not to being 'Christian' or to being part of Christianity." Maybe Bonhoeffer is correct when he coined the term "religionless Christianity." (p. 219) He said that the term "Christian" has been so distorted by the institution of the church and required belief systems that there might be a more appropriate designation. For some Christians my current belief system will not be accepted as "Christian." Depending upon one's definition of Christian, I speculate, as Pastor Robin Meyers of Oklahoma City United Church of Christ asked himself one Sunday morning after delivering the sermon at his church, "Am I a Christian?" This question is not uncommon. Catholic theologian Paul Knitter also asked "Am I still a Christian?" (p. ix) He admitted that for most of his adult life he has struggled with the big questions, like God and Jesus. I often think I'd rather be considered a follower of "The Way," as early Christians were called—followers of Jesus.

While the foundation for the evolution of my faith goes back to my childhood and the tumultuous 1960's when I was a college student for most of the decade, I did not take any action on those concerns until I was almost 50 years old. Years of college exposed me to the ideas of great thinkers, philosophers, and theologians and I realized that truth and the examination of truth can be found in places other than just the Bible and the church. While I was bothered by the misinformation I had come to believe as preached by the evangelical/fundamentalist Christian church, I did not act on those concerns.

Upon completing my doctorate from Springfield College in 1968, I accepted my first job teaching at South Dakota State University and stayed for 6 years. I then worked at ORU as a faculty member, department chair, and dean of a college for 14 years; then on to Arkansas State University for 5 years; and finally at age 50 to Northern Arizona University (NAU) until retirement at age 65—40 years of college teaching. Until I went to Arizona, I had repressed the theological concerns that I had. I went about raising a family, developing a professional career, pursuing some financial security, and enjoying the benefits of my job, family, and resources. I was happy and enjoyed life.

There was, however, always a gnawing feeling, that something was not right about my fundamentalist faith. Growing up, the most common argument given me whenever I would question something strange in the Bible, was there are many things we don't understand, but we just accept it since it is the "Word of God." Or, don't ever question the "Word of God." Dan Brown, author of bestselling books *The Da Vinci Code* and *Angels and Demons* stated that when as a high school student he posed such questions to his pastor, he was told, "nice boys don't ask such questions." The Bible was seen as literal, factual, infallible, and without error. End of discussion.

When I was a child that answer seemed all right. It is a lot easier to just believe something or ignore it. Over the past 20 years, I have no longer been able to "just believe" or "ignore" things such as the ethnic cleansing, the many strange laws that appear in the Old Testament, and the lack of evidence to support the many promises in the Bible. It seemed that the choice I had was to believe that God endorses ethnic cleansing, slavery, violence, and condones other strange behaviors or to change my view of the Bible. Initially, neither choice was comforting. In time, the choice became obvious and compelling.

Radical Grace, a publication of the Center for Action and Contemplation, devoted the fall 2010 publication to "The Two Halves of Life." Richard Rohr writes that the first half of life is creating a "container" for one's life and the second half of life is to find the actual "contents" for the container. Decisions about what is really significant become an important part of the second half of life. A key part of the second half is discovering "what parts of the first half should I hold on to and what parts should I let go of because they no longer serve me well." It becomes a time for "shedding rather than holding on." It is a time for "putting aside childish things." And so this has been for me. Now the question is, "what beliefs do I put aside, what do I keep, and what do I modify if it is kept."

It is important to note that this is an ongoing process, a conversation. In her excellent book *The Great Emergence: How Christianity is Changing and Why*, Phyllis Tickle puts into perspective the changes that she sees taking place in Christianity over the past 50 years and especially today. She writes that owing to the advancement of knowledge and science over the past 100 plus years, "literalism [of the Bible] based on inerrancy could not survive the blow (though it would die a slow and painful death); and without inerrancy-based literalism…where now is our authority?" (p. 82) She suggests the authority rests in a "conversation" among those in the Christian "community." (p. 153) This discussion within a community is perhaps the new authority since "…in and through community lies the salvation of the world." (Peck, p. 21)

This conversation has been one of the most rewarding parts of my life over the past 20 years. I have sought out other "seeking souls" and we have read books and articles by some of the great thinkers and theologians and shared our thoughts and struggles with many ideas. Initially, an especially excellent book/bible study I had was with 12 to 16 persons in Flagstaff, AZ. These were all wonderful Christians who regularly attended church, prayed, sought for a personal relationship with God, and served others. As I was struggling over my belief in the Bible as the written, literal Word of God and was ready to "let it go," one evening while studying *The Heart of Christianity* by Marcus Borg, I asked the group if they believed the Bible was the Word of God? As each shared their thoughts, it was 100% NO. I couldn't believe it. How could these wonderful Christians not believe that the Bible was the absolute Word of God? This conversation with people I trusted and valued gave me permission for the first time to accept what I had been feeling for years. I can still be a committed Christian and "let go" of the belief that the Bible is the Word of God. It was an evening of liberation. No longer was I under the law of an obsolete belief. No longer did I need to worship the Bible as an Idol. This conversation has continued with another committed group of Christian seekers in Colorado where we moved upon retirement in 2008.

While I have greatly enjoyed the concept of "conversation," it is important to note I am not a theologian. I am not trained or educated as one. What I know and express comes from reading scriptures, personal experience, reason, the study of classic theologians, and conversations. Therefore, what I have read and studied is very important (see "sources and resources" for some of what I've read in this journey). I have not wanted to build a faith on "shared ignorance" or a prejudicial belief system.

My observations, unfortunately, have been that many of the evan-gelical/fundamentalist pastors and evangelists that I have known and from whom I've learned have had limited theological training. They teach and spread their beliefs with a great deal of authority and charisma. They attract many followers. As Borg puts it, outside of mainline denominations, we have the least educated clergy in the world! This, and the fact that "self-ordained, uneducated/entrepre-neurial ministers" tend to start very conservative churches and dom-inate Christian radio and TV could be the reason why fundamentalism often gets the upper hand over more progressive views. I had firsthand experience of that from my 14 years at Oral Roberts University. Oral Roberts, as well as many of the leading evangelists and preachers who came to campus to speak, had limited theological training. I spent the first 40 plus years of my life reading and listening only to those with limited theological education.

When I wanted to re-evaluate my beliefs, including reconsidering the Bible as the Word of God, I did so by attempting to read and learn from those regarded by their peers as strong academic scholars of the Bible and of the early Christian church. I read what academic scholars and well-educated theologians were saying, not preachers who had a bias in their message and limited theological education. These readings and conversations have led me to accept the writings of those who advocate "Progressive Christianity." I have also been influenced by "Process Theology," which attempts to make sense of God and Christianity in a modern world (Mesle). In the interest of brevity and simplicity, in the following sections I will summarize briefly my current belief and understanding relative to God, Jesus, prayer, heaven, and discuss the idea of progressive Christianity. The view presented satisfies and makes the most sense to me. (For a more thorough discussion on these topics refer to the sources and resources at the end of the book.)

Where were you when I laid the earth's foundation? Tell me, if you understand.

Job 38:4

Chapter Fifteen

A REVISED UNDERSTANDING OF BASIC BELIEFS:
God, Jesus, Prayer, and Heaven

Good. I previously thought of God as a Being dwelling somewhere in the heavens surrounded by angels and other heavenly beings. This God was a personal God who had the hairs on my head numbered and had a plan for my life. In about 7 literal days, some 10,000 years ago, he (of course God was a he) created the universe as it exists today; including all the plants, animals, and humans. My job was to seek God to find this plan and his will for my life. This God from time to time intervened in the affairs of man. God regularly rewarded or punished humans. The habits, likes, and dislikes of God seemingly were well known to the pastors and teachers in the evangelical churches I attended. They would often share messages they had heard directly from God. Today, I believe any image of God that we have is a man-made image.

While some claim to have much apparent knowledge about God, those who have spent their entire life studying God are the most willing to admit that they really understand little about God, and in fact admit little can be known. John Shelby Spong echo's the statement found in Job when he writes, "Whatever God is, God is surely beyond the boundaries of human life. So the more specific we are about God, the less accurate we probably are. A human being cannot escape the boundaries or perspective of what it means to be human and therefore can never define or describe what it means to be God. I wonder why it is that we not only continue to try to do the impossible, but even continue to persecute those who disagree with our definition or description." *(Eternal Life: A New Vision*, p. 146)

Bawer expressed similar thoughts relative to the concept of God. He stated, "Tillich's concept of 'God beyond God'… his recognition that there is something humanly unknowable is an insight that made immediate sense to me…why can't we simply accept with humility that we don't know all there is to know about God and that we may actually be wrong about some of the things we think we know." (p. 46)

Pearson, asked himself a question; "Does the God I've heard about and preached all my life exist?" (p. xii) "I used to think," writes Pearson, "I had to believe in God, I had to 'know God,' I had to study the Bible to know God and understand God. Now, for the first time in my life, I don't feel an obligation to literally know God…I find the most satisfactory view of God, as a force and/or source that is beyond human understanding." (p. xviii) Pearson writes that God cannot be limited or defined or necessarily known. "God is really just our word for that which cannot be named or fully grasped." (p. 134-147)

Knitter, drawing from both his Roman Catholic background as well as his examination of Buddhism, says that God is "…indefinable, incomprehensible, unspeakable…can never be defined." (p. 53, 56) He makes an interesting observation that because of the mysteriousness of God, "religion offers equal attraction to brilliant minds and to crackpots." (p. 54) He concludes that since God is a mystery, "beyond human intelligence…trying to describe God distracts from what we can do and need to do: figure out how to deal with suffering, how to live peacefully and compassionately. Do that first, and then there might be time to entertain questions, if that is needed…about God." (p. 60-61) Mesle echoes the idea expressed by Knitter. As a theologian, his concern is when he theorizes about the nature of God, it might distract readers from what is really important. For him, our focus should be on what we know and how we can address the misery in our world and the welfare of our planet. (p. 67) Mesle discusses the concept of "theistic naturalism" which I can relate to.

Two other authors that express the view that God is mystery are Thomas Keating (2009) and Phillip Yancey (2000). The former said, "God is the ultimate mystery. You cannot know God but you can appreciate God." Yancey wrote, "the older I get the more comfortable I am with mystery." Voltaire, who was a skeptic and Deist and perhaps the undisputed leader of the Age of Enlightenment, made an interesting observation. "If God did not exist, it would be necessary to invent him." This is an echo of what Homer wrote in the Odyssey "all men need gods." Maybe humans have a great need to believe in a God; something that gives meaning to the universe, life, and death. In this process of believing, maybe humans have a need to describe a god that can be put in a box and controlled. In her book, *A History of God*, Armstrong writes, "In the beginning, human beings created God." (p. 3) Originally this god (called the Sky God among other names) created all things and lived afar in the heavens. Throughout history, humans have continued to create "gods" as one was replaced by a more "attractive" god that related to the changing culture. The gods of ancient tribes were not unlike the God described in the Bible and central to Judaism, Christianity, and Islam.

I am comfortable with the mystery of God. While throughout history humans have sought to create a god in their own image, I am content that I really can't know or understand God. I agree with Spong that the more we attempt to explain or describe God, more than likely the less accurate is our understanding. St. Augustine in the third-century said, "if you think you understand it, it is not God." (Smith, p. 144) I enjoy conversations with other seeking souls on the nature of God, God's role in pain and suffering, and God's interaction with the world. While I enjoy these conversations, I accept that

I cannot know. I can honor and respect God; I conceivably can experience God; but I will never know if I am experiencing God or if my experience is the result of my own emotions and perceptions.

For me, the closest I can come to understand this mystery of God is to explore his creation; study nature, the earth, and the vastness of the universe. The Hubble Space Telescope has revealed that almost 98% of the vast universe is invisible. Francis Collins, former director of the International Human Genome Project, was the lead scientist to study and map the Human DNA sequence revealing a code 3 billion letters long. Collins wrote, "We are learning the language in which God created life. We are gaining evermore awe for the complexity, the beauty, and the wonder of God's most divine and sacred gift...we have caught the first glimpse of our own instruction book, previously known only to God." (p. 2-3)

Jane Goodall, world famous primatologist, at age 76 was asked by *Readers Digest* (Sept 2010) if she believed in God. Her answer: "I don't have any idea of who or what God is. But I do believe in some great spiritual power. I don't know what to call it. I feel it particularly when I'm out in nature. It's just something that's bigger and stronger than what I am or what anybody is. I feel it. And it's enough for me."

This speaks to me. Having studied anatomy and physiology of the human organism and having spent much time in nature, the mountains, forests, deserts, and canyons, I am ever amazed at God's creation. When I am alone in nature, as I take in its magnificence, I am reminded of my insignificance. Borg, a fellow student at Concordia, writes, "in God we live and move and have our being." (Acts 17:28) Borg's writings have expressed, with theological insight, thoughts that I've had for years. His spiritual journey and writings have given me a Christian faith that I can believe. I especially relate to his analogy of the fish in water. A fish is both in water which gives it its life and energy as well as there is water in the fish which is also essential for its life. God is all around us and God also dwells within us; the very breath we breathe. God is, as Karen Armstrong has stated, the "all encompassing spirit," as Paul Tillich describes the "ground of being" or as Paul writes, God is "above all, through all, and in all." (Ephesians 4:6) I believe we honor the mystery of God when in silence we meditate upon God's greatness, when we show our love and respect and our worship of God by our care of God's creation, the earth and sky, our love of neighbor, being passionate about what Jesus was passionate about, our care for the "least of these among us," and our passion for justice and peace. We demonstrate our love of God when we seek to provide food, shelter, clothing, education, health care, dignity, and compassion for all persons.

Jacobsen and Sawatsky (p. 130) write that when we love God, we find that we also necessarily love others and as we love others in some sense we are also loving God. This is the heart of what they say is "gracious Christianity" which sounds very similar to progressive Christianity. They declare that this is the creed of Jesus, the Christian's rule of life.

In concluding this section on God, Thomas Paine, in his pamphlet/book *The Age of Reason*, published in the 1790's, defines God as the "first cause" of all creation. He, asks "Is there a Word of God?" He answers with, "The Word of God is the creation we behold; and it is a word, which no human invention can counterfeit or alter, that God speaketh universally to man…it is an ever existing original, which every man can read. It cannot be forged; it cannot be suppressed…it preaches to all nations and to all worlds; and this Word of God reveals to man all that is necessary for man to know of God…search not the book called the scripture, which any human hand might make, but search the scripture called the Creation." (Chapter 9)

Jesus. I previously thought of Jesus primarily for his role in atonement. That is, he died on the cross to somehow atone for our sins, and if we accepted and believed in this sacrificial act, we'd be forgiven of our sins, accepted by God, saved, and would spend eternity in heaven. I was comfortable with that belief and worshiped Jesus as my savior. Today, I do not believe this is an accurate picture of the nature of Jesus, and I find I'm in good company.

To be sure, Jesus is central to Christianity. "Christians find the ultimate disclosure of God in a person and not in a book, Jesus is more central than the Bible." (*The Heart of Christianity*, p. 80-81) Since little can be found in the literature during the time of Jesus, almost all of what we know about Jesus comes from the four gospels. It is important to understand, as discussed by Borg, these gospels are testimonies. "They are a mixture of historical memory and metaphorical narrative." (p. 84) Some of the events literally happened and some did not. They were written 30 to 70 years after the death of Jesus. As Meyers states, "We know that the gospels were written in the last third of the first century, and that they are not historical accounts, but testimonies of faith." (*Saving Jesus from the Church*. p. 22) John, who wrote his gospel some 60 years after the death of Jesus, made it clear that he was trying to convince his readers that Jesus is the Messiah. (John 20:31) The key to our understanding is what we can learn from the life and death of Jesus and to be a follower of Jesus.

But what Jesus are we to follow? Meyers writes that Christianity has taken the easy route of accepting Jesus as Christ and believing in him in order to get benefits. That is much easier than following the way of Jesus, becoming his disciple. The focus of his book is that we need to stop worshipping Christ and begin following Jesus. Meyers issues a call to follow Jesus since a focus on doctrines and beliefs divide but discipleship brings us together. "We have come to a moment in human history when the message of the Sermon on the

Mount could indeed save us, but it can no longer be heard above the din of dueling doctrines. Consider this: there is not a single word in that sermon about what to believe, only words about what to do. It is a behavioral manifesto." (p. 14) On the other hand, the Apostles Creed or the Nicene Creed, which represent the official doctrine of the Christian church, do not have a single word about what to do, only what to believe. In these creeds, the life and teachings of Jesus is relegated to a comma! To the early Christians being a Christian was following Jesus, following "the way." Today being a Christian has evolved into accepting a belief system in order to receive benefits promised by some church. "The divine Savior image is now so exclusively the message of evangelical and fundamentalist Christianity that the Sermon on the Mount seems almost superfluous." (p. 19)

Nolan (1992) describes the life and teachings of Jesus before individuals in the third and fourth centuries revised his teachings into an organized religion with doctrines and other beliefs and in the process lost the basic principles and message of Jesus. White (2004) and Harris (2008) go even further and describe how Christianity, as a religion, has significantly distorted the life and teachings of Jesus.

Bourgeault (2008), as well as Farley (2011), emphasize that we must remember two things about Jesus. First, he lived in a Middle Eastern culture 2000 years ago. It resembled little of our Western culture of today. Second, there was considerable debate while Jesus lived and especially in the 200-300 years after his death as to "who was Jesus?" The New Testament we have today that presents the stories of Jesus came about as the result of much debate and controversy. After the church leaders voted on the Bible contents, Bishop Athanasius in 367 ordered that all the writings that were not in the final version of the Bible be destroyed and that those who adhered to these writings were branded as heretics. Apparently, some of the writings were preserved by burying them and were found in 1948.

For the past 60 years, Biblical scholars have carefully examined these documents.

What scholars find is that while the orthodoxy of Christianity saw Jesus as the Savior, the early Christians whose writings were destroyed saw Jesus not so much as the "lamb of God that takes away the sins of the world," but rather as a wisdom teacher. Bourgeault stresses that Jesus was not just a humble carpenter, but, was well educated and full of knowledge and wisdom. He challenged the religious leaders of his day with "razor edge brilliance." (p. 27) Central for us today, is to seek the wisdom of Jesus. For Bourgeault, this is best done through the practice of meditation as it is "the cornerstone of the wisdom encounter with Christ." (p. 141)

Girzone is a Catholic priest who wrote his first book "Joshua" upon retiring from the church in 1985. He paints a very warm portrait of Jesus who says if we really followed him, our life and communities would be extremely different. They would be more caring, loving, compassionate, and the focus would be on "the least of these among us." While organized Christianity is quick to condemn anyone who does not share their vision, "you never see Jesus criticizing anyone except the organized religion of his day." (*A Portrait of Jesus*. p. 35) While organized religion was focused on feasts, rituals, and obeying the law, "for Jesus it was loving God, caring for people, and appreciating the wonderful creation God has blessed us with." (p. 53)

Borg summarizes what Jesus was like during his lifetime. Jesus emphasized that we were to be "born again" or "transformed" from a focus on ourselves to a focus on others. Our central goal in life, he says, is to love God and love others; and we love God by the degree to which we love and give ourselves to others. He was a "radical critic of the domination system of his time that channeled wealth to the few and poverty to the many." (*The Heart of Christianity*, p. 91) He was a movement initiator, attracted followers, associated with the marginalized and outcasts, and challenged the social boundaries of his day. Ultimately, "he was killed because of his politics, because of his passion for God's justice." (p. 92) Borg makes a strong theological and historical case that the death of Jesus was not "for our sins" and salvation means transformation rather than being heaven bound.

Knitter, like Borg, writes about the "distinctive life of Jesus who had a preferential love for those people in every society who have been stepped on, pushed aside, neglected, or exploited. Jesus embodied this preferential, pressing love for the poor and hungry and cast-aside even to the point of dying like one of them…Jesus suffers not only for the victims of the world…but suffers like them…if we are not responding to the suffering of others…we most likely are following a misleading path." (p. 126)

Elaine Pagels (2012) writes how when Rome conquered other nations during the time of Jesus, the people of the captured countries were required to worship Roman gods in addition to their own gods. However, the Jews of Israel refused and rather than require them to worship the Roman gods, Rome made an accommodation for them with the agreement that the Jews could worship in their historic way as long as they were loyal to Rome. When Jesus came along, he rejected this arrangement by challenging the religious leaders of his day. That challenge upset the religious leaders as well as Rome and resulted in the execution of Jesus.

Did Jesus rise from the dead after his death? Phillip Yancey wonders why, as the Bible records, Jesus appeared after the resurrection to just a limited number of people and those were only his friends. He writes that many have looked at the evidence of the resurrection and have found it impossible to believe. He goes on to say, "I admit that at a very deep level I want the Easter story to be true…I suppose you could say I want to believe in fairy tales." (*The Jesus I Never Knew.* p. 218) Perhaps debates over whether or not he was raised from the dead are distractions from following the life and teachings of Jesus.

For most of my life I have been troubled by the doctrine of atonement. I was glad in my studies to find I am not alone. Meyers writes, "According to this dominant view (i.e. the doctrine of the atonement), we are born with original sin, damned, and helpless to overcome that sin and gain eternal life unless an adequate sacrifice is made. This can't be an animal or even an imperfect human but must be a 'perfect' sacrifice provided by God in the form of a perfect human being (the Christ). He is the substitute victim who takes on the punishment deserved by humanity that is required for restoration and forgiveness by a 'loving' God. This raises an obvious and deeply disturbing question: 'is God so implacable that he demands a victim and so unjust that he does not mind that the victim is innocent?'" Meyers goes on to write, "Think what this view says about God. First, God must not be both all-powerful and all-loving, or God would not require such a sacrifice in order to be restored to his own creation. Second, if this 'had to happen,' then we are dealing with a deity who not only must play by our rules, but is, at best, capable of being bribed or, at worst, guilty of divine child abuse."

Meyers continues, "Serious study of the bible reveals that no crucifixion story existed for at least forty years after the death of Jesus… all we know for certain is that it happened." (p. 56) The crucifixion story was written in the 8th decade. "The most prominent understanding is that his death was sacrificial, even though the fully formed doctrine of the blood atonement did not appear until after the first millennium, or about 900 years ago. Yet this idea now dominates popular Christianity and must be rejected if the church is to survive." (p. 80+)

In summary, for me the good news Jesus brought was that devotion to God did not require a specific belief or precise religious practice; rather it was radical and simple: to love God and love your neighbor. Any requirements beyond loving God and neighbor are man-made. At the age of 77, Thomas Jefferson created the "Jefferson Bible" by cutting out of the Bible what he felt were the "embellishments" and kept the words only of Jesus. He described the teachings of Jesus as the most "sublime and benevolent code of morals ever offered to man."

I am reminded of the paper I wrote as an undergraduate student at Concordia College almost 50 years ago on the topic "Was Abraham Lincoln a Christian?" The topic was chosen for a theology class since Lincoln never joined a church. When asked why not, he replied, "When the sole requirement for membership is to love God and love my neighbor, that church will I join." I believe Lincoln was right. The question, "what would Jesus do?" should be our guide. It is a much greater challenge to follow Jesus than to confess to some statement of beliefs. Making a confession of faith is the easy way out. Following the teachings of Jesus indeed requires doing something, often something you'd rather not do. It requires sacrifice, giving, seeking out the disenfranchised, and challenging religious fundamentalism of our day as Jesus did in his day. To be a disciple of Jesus is an onerous task. No wonder this form of Christianity is not popular and the Christianity of prosperity, healing, and statement of beliefs is so ubiquitous.

Prayer. I have been influenced by what Knitter writes about prayer. He indicates that prayer is the "practice" of one's faith. Unfortunately, he says that prayer all too often follows the parental model. We get what we need from our parents. Most of our prayers are conversations with God asking for something. We petition a God we perceive to be "out there" to intervene in the affairs on earth. It involves a lot of talking and often pleading. This concept was driven home while on the faculty at ORU. A new dean of the Theology School, Larry Lea, was hired. He had developed and promoted a one hour daily prayer process that followed the example of the Lord's Prayer. After learning the process of this praying, for more than 6 months I faithfully got up early each morning before breakfast and work and followed Lea's prayer format. Its focus was on thanking God for the benefits of his covenant with us, making faith declarations such as God being my shepherd, my healer, my protector; then praying for the will of God to take place in my family, my church, my nation; praying and believing God will prosper me; praying for forgiveness for myself and others, and finally praying for God's protection for me. The prayer was primarily my talking to God, petitioning God to intervene here on earth, and getting me "fired up" that God was looking out for me and taking care of me. Reflecting on this experience, perhaps it was a useful time of prayer, but I wonder. It seemed like it was too much talk and not much listening or taking action.

As Knitter complains, in the practice of prayer, we talk too much! "If the Divine is truly a Mystery that is beyond all human comprehension, beyond all human ideas and words, then any spiritual practice must make room—lots of room—for the practice of silence. And that is what is missing in Christian practice." (p. 137) It is through the study of Buddhism that Knitter suggests we can modify and strengthen the traditional practice of prayer to the practice of meditation, or as Father Thomas Keating (2009) calls it, "centering prayer." Keating further writes, "God's first language is silence. Everything else is translation."

Knitter suggests that our prayers should be more in the form of meditation; and he discusses two types of meditation in the Buddhist tradition…meditation that promotes wisdom and meditation that promotes compassion. This particularly resonates with me since my belief is that the heart of a Christian life is "loving God and loving my neighbor." A prayer life should be focused on accomplishing those two critical behaviors. Meditation (prayer) has a *focus on wisdom* and its practice is to be quiet; don't think about anything, and totally relax so that you will be sensitive to what the "Sacred, Spirit, God, Mystery" is "telling" you which goes beyond words and thoughts. Knitter suggests a new sacrament…the Sacrament of Silence (meditation) to be practiced both privately in our homes and in our church services. "If Mystery is the goal and content of all religion, then silence (meditation) is a necessary means to let Mystery speak." (p. 154) Perhaps we can learn from the Quaker tradition in which their worship services are conducted in silence.

Meditation (prayer) that has a *focus on compassion* is directed toward my becoming more compassionate towards the needs of others and not petitioning God to take care of the problem. It is quietly reflecting on the needs of my family, my neighbors, and others and seeking guidance on how I can best demonstrate my love and concern for others. It is sending my love and concern to others. It is then following through with actions that reflect compassion and kindness. As Robinson states, "my own experience is that I am really praying for people, agonizing with God for them, precisely as I meet them and really give my soul to them." (p. 97-99)

Summarizing my thoughts on prayer, in keeping with the concept of "love God and love neighbor," our prayer life should first be one of meditation with a *focus on wisdom*. We quietly sit in silence listening for Mystery to "speak." We listen for thoughts and ideas and are sensitive to the Spirit that is within us. Secondly, our prayer life should be one of meditation with a *focus on compassion*. As we become aware of the needs of others and engage with them, we are really praying for them, agonizing with God for them, precisely as we meet them and really give ourselves to them. Our prayers are to give us focus for action. Our prayers (meditation) are not seeking some divine intervention, rather, personal courage for us to act with wisdom and compassion.

Heaven. My previous concept of heaven was that it is a wonderful place where I will live after I die. Not everyone will get there, in fact, most would not. I saw heaven as a place created by God as a reward for those who had accepted Jesus as their personal savior. The focus of life on earth was to prepare for heaven. According to a 2012 Gallup Poll, 85% of all Americans believe in some sort of life after death. Interestingly, the type of afterlife varies widely. (Meacham)

Nowhere is the influence of religion more persuasive than the idea of the afterlife. The institution of the church defines the route by which a person attains life after death and controls the process. The church administers baptism or dedication as a child; offers religious education to children and confirmation; controls the "sacrament" of marriage; defines what sin is and requires confession in order to receive forgiveness required for the attainment of heaven; expects a 10% contribution for their services; and administers the funeral that provides the comfort to those who remain of the assurance that the person is now in heaven. While other religions may have a different route to their version of heaven, such as re-incarnation, etc, the control process is the same.

While I would like to believe there is a heaven and hope I'd go there, Borg expresses a thought I have about heaven. He writes, "If I were to make a list of Christianity's 10 worst contributions to religion, on that list would be popular Christianity's emphasis on the afterlife." (*The Heart of Christianity*, p. 171-72) He says, first, when the focus is on the afterlife, religion becomes a set of rules and regulations in order to get to heaven. Second, religion becomes a "we/they," the saved and the unsaved. It divides rather than unites people. Thirdly, when the focus is on the afterlife, there is often a lack of concern for this life and the need to improve this world. He then reviews the different concepts of the afterlife and heaven, and concludes that no one has any valid idea of life beyond death. I am comfortable that the God "in whom we live and move and have our being" is in charge. What more do we need to know? So, why focus any time on trying to develop a "theology" of the afterlife? Create whatever dream you want, whatever gives you comfort.

Knitter discusses the Buddhist concept of the afterlife and the various Christian concepts of the afterlife (heaven). When we talk about the afterlife, he says we really "don't know what we are talking about." (p. 75) What happens beyond death is totally a mystery. While it is comforting, for some, to think of being reunited with family, living in eternal bliss, being spared from hell [if we followed the correct beliefs and practices of our religion], the bottom line is we really don't know. As I've discussed and come to believe, the Bible is not the "Word of God," rather it is man's attempt to write about the unknown. Therefore, any discussion of heaven found in the Bible is nothing more than man's invention. I think the Buddhists perhaps have it right. Since the afterlife is a mystery, focus on the here and now…this moment. Knitter concludes by saying, "…in the end, I just trust. I trust after my death…there will be life. Or in the words of Julian of Norwich, all manner of things will be well…Cherish the Mystery." (p. 90-91)

Carl Sagan, the outstanding astrophysicist said, "I would love to believe that when I die I will live again. But much as I want to believe that, despite ancient and worldwide cultural traditions that assert an afterlife, I know of nothing to suggest that it is more than wishful thinking. Far better is to look death in the eye and be grateful every day for the brief but magnificent opportunity that life provides."

In summary, of course, I'd love to see my family and other loved ones in heaven. Of course, I hope that there is a wonderful life to come when this one ends. But to focus one's attention on the afterlife, if there is any, is a distraction from this life where our center of attention needs to be. I have faith in the Mystery of what lies ahead. I need not think or dwell on it. Iris Dement captured my thoughts in her wonderful song, "Let the Mystery Be."

Everybody's wonderin' what and where they all came from.
Everybody's worryin' 'bout where they're gonna go when the whole thing's done.
Some say they're goin' to a place called Glory and I ain't saying it ain't a fact.
Some say once you're gone you're gone forever,
and some say you're gonna come back.
Some say you rest in the arms of the Savior if in sinful ways you lack.
But no one knows for certain and so it's all the same to me.
I think I'll just let the mystery be.
I think I'll just let the mystery be.

When the song of the angels is stilled,
When the star in the sky is gone,
When kings and princes are home,
When shepherds are back with their flocks,
The work of Christmas begins:
To find the lost,
To heal the broken,
To feed the hungry,
To release the prisoners,
To rebuild the nations,
To bring peace among people,
To make music in the heart.

—"The Work of Christmas" by Howard Thurman

Chapter Sixteen

FINDING A HOME IN PROGRESSIVE CHRISTIANITY

As I evolved in my theology about God, Jesus, prayer, and heaven, my Christian faith is not the same as my child or young adulthood. I've let go of many beliefs and now feel at home with the concept of "Progressive Christianity."

"Progressive Christianity," while being a relatively new term, is as old as the first century. A number of current authors have provided their description. Phyllis Tickle describes a progressive Christian as someone who wants to stay within Christianity but get rid of the dogma-based ideas and doctrinally restricted beliefs. Eric Elnes says, a progressive Christian is "anyone who believes that loving God, neighbor, and self" is the heart of being a Christian. It is following the life and teachings of Jesus; that's it. All the doctrines, beliefs, and creeds are man-infused distractions, part of institutions but not the heart of being a Christian. For a progressive Christian the focus is not so much on personal salvation in order to get to heaven as it is having a focus on caring for the disenfranchised; as Howard Thurman might say, it is conducting the "work of Christmas."

Peters and Hinson-Hasty (2008) present a general overview of the concept of a "progressive Christian," which they state is grounded in the teachings of the Bible and especially Jesus. Micah 6:8 reminds us that "what does the lord require of you but to do justice, to love mercy, and walk humbly with your God." Luke 4:18 describes the mission of Jesus was "...to bring good news to the poor...release to the captives...sight to the blind, to let the oppressed go free...." His life and teachings demonstrated that we are to resist unjust laws (such as his healing on the Sabbath); that we are to love ghbor as ourselves which requires hospitality to strangers, enemies, and those in need (Good Samaritan in Luke 10); and loving God requires us to feed the hungry, give drink to the thirsty, welcome the stranger, clothe the naked, care for the sick, and visit with prisoners. (Matthew 25:34-40) "Jesus' life and work are the model for living faithfully in a world marked by sin, greed, and brokenness. Living as Christians in a pluralistic world requires that we work together with people of other faiths and the larger communities to address the social problems that hinder people from living lives of fullness and integrity." (Peters, p. xiv)

Additionally, a "progressive Christian is one who draws upon a variety of rich sources (Christian teachings and tradition, science, experience, social sciences, philosophy, and teachings from other wisdom traditions) to better understand society's problems so that we can work in collaboration with others to help our society, our world, and the church to move toward God's vision of a new earth." (Peters, p. xiv) While "progressive Christians support charitable actions to meet the immediate needs of people in crisis, their deeper concern is to transform the social systems and economic structures of society that marginalize people and the natural world." (Peters, p. xiv) Jesus was not executed for his good deeds, rather because he challenged the religious, economic, and political systems of his day.

The vision of the Center for Progressive Christianity, is to encourage churches to focus their attention on those for whom organized religion has proven to be "ineffectual, irrelevant, or repressive." They define progressive Christians as individuals who: (ProgressiveChristianity.org, "The 8 Points." Accessed June 24, 2012)

1. Believe that following the path and teachings of Jesus can lead to an awareness and experience of the Sacred and the Oneness and Unity of all life;

2. Affirm that the teachings of Jesus provide but one of many ways

to experience the Sacredness and Oneness of life, and that we can draw from diverse sources of wisdom in our spiritual journey;

3. Seek community that is inclusive of ALL people, including but not limited to:
   a. Conventional Christians and questioning skeptics,
   b. Believers and agnostics,
   c. Women and men,
   d. Those of all sexual orientations and gender identities,
   e. Those of all classes and abilities;
4. Know that the way we behave towards one another is the fullest expression of what we believe;
5. Find grace in the search for understanding and believe there is more value in questioning than in absolutes;
6. Strive for peace and justice among all people;
7. Strive to protect and restore the integrity of our earth; and
8. Commit to a path of life-long learning, compassion, and selfless love.

To these guidelines, Borg adds two more key aspects of Progressive Christianity:
1. Focus on this life more than on the next life;
2. Accept a non-literal reading of the Bible.

A progressive Christian, according to Peters and Hinson-Hasty (2008), has a distinctive worldview that is rooted in three principles:
1. Christian faithfulness requires public action by churches and people of faith. "Christianity is not simply a personal and private matter between an individual and God; it is also about community responsibility and faithfulness in public life—social, political, and economic...as Christians living in a democracy, we have a

special and unique opportunity to work together to confront the problems that are shaping social patterns and practices in destructive ways.... Christianity is not an individualistic faith; rather, Christians are called to live in community and to be active in the world in ways that witness to our faith in all areas of our lives." Progressive Christians seek to address problems through; 1) scripture, 2) tradition, 3) science/reason, and 4) lived experiences. (p. xix)

2. Christian social witness and public action should correspond to accepted practices of deliberative democracies. Since many people will not share our theological claims, we must modify the first principle to state that our social action and public action should correspond to accepted practices in a deliberative democracy. "Thus, while our faith motivates us to act in the world, we must develop language and the moral arguments that allow us to debate with and enlist the support from those who may not share our faith commitments but do support democratic discourse in a pluralistic world." (p. xx)

3. The cause of social problems is often structural or systemic. Social problems are not exclusively the fault of the individual but are often caused by structural or system failure. The United States currently has the dominant view and obsession with an individualism that views success or failures as the sole responsibility of the individual. This view is threatening to "tear the fabric of our community apart. We stand on the shoulders of others—our parents, teachers, ministers, mentors, friends, families, and all the other people who have contributed to our success and well-being in the world." (p. xxi) The welfare reform legislation, the Personal Responsibility and Work Opportunity Reconciliation Act of 1996 was based upon an "assumed individualistic cause of poverty—that poor people are lazy." Census data of 2005 indicated that

37 million people in the US were living below the poverty line and of these, 60% had at least one family member employed. While some quote "you will always have the poor with you" (John 12:8) to justify the existence of poverty, the overwhelming teachings of the Bible and especially Jesus indicates this was not one of his teachings. With the ever-widening gap between the rich and the poor and the multitude of problems that this gap creates, many people feel overwhelmed. There is a desperate need for "people who will see the world and their role in it in a new way." (p. xxi)

How one should live one's life has been examined and pondered since the arrival of humankind on earth. Throughout recorded history individuals with special insight and wisdom have been born into various and diverse cultures. Around 500 BCE in India, Gautama Buddha, frustrated with the Hindu tradition of spiritual practices, left his family and wealth and pursued a more effective way to seek God. After 6 years of study and extensive meditation, he achieved "enlightenment." He then began his life of teaching the path to enlightenment. These teachings contain much wisdom, and after his death, his followers wrote down many of his sayings. During his lifetime, he never suggested that he was Divine or should be worshipped, but centuries later, some of his followers do consider him a god—perhaps not unlike Jesus. Today there are about 400 million who follow Buddhist teachings.

At about the same time in China, there lived a wise teacher, politician, and philosopher, Confucius. His teachings emphasized justice, morality, harmony, and social relationships. He was one of the early teachers who espoused the principle "do not do to others what you do not want done to yourself." Similar to the teachings of Jesus, Confucius taught by using allusions and parables. His teachings require context and examination to be understood. His influence on far eastern thought and philosophy was profound. Again, he did not try to develop a religion; rather his focus was on the morals and ethics of living life on earth. Today there are about 400 million who follow these ancient Chinese teachings.

Over 2000 years ago, into a world not unlike our own, with political corruption and a religious establishment deep with its laws, greed, and authority, was born a man called John. He lived a simple life, followed a strange diet, wore weird clothes, and lived away from the public. He called the religious leaders "brood of vipers" and challenged people to repent of their sins and change their ways. When people asked him "what should we do," he simply said that those with plenty of clothes and food should share their food and clothing with those who have none. To the tax collectors he said don't collect more than you are required and to the soldiers his advice was don't extort money, don't accuse people falsely, and be content with your pay. He didn't lecture them on doctrine, going to church, or the law. He gave them seemingly simple advice for people who sought repentance for their ways. (see Luke 3:7-14)

John spoke of another person who would follow him who had far more important things to say and do than he. Shortly thereafter, Jesus, the person he was speaking of, arrived on the scene with the announcement "the spirit of the Lord is upon me because he has anointed me to preach the good news to the poor. He has sent me to proclaim freedom for the prisoners and recovery of sight for the blind, to release the oppressed." (Luke 4-18) With this statement, Jesus announced his life's purpose and mission. The accounts of the life of Jesus as recorded in the books of Matthew, Mark, Luke, and John document that he did exactly what he announced in his mission statement. As John did before him, he spoke out against the laws and superiority of the religious establishment and announced the "good news." To please God required the fulfillment of only two laws (since all other laws were dependent upon these two)...love the Lord with all your heart, soul, and mind and your neighbor as yourself. (Matthew 22:36-40) That's it! Very simple! That's the good news. With John and Jesus, I too reject many of the rules, beliefs, and dogmas of organized religion and aspire to the simplicity of a life loving God and neighbor.

When John was in prison, discouraged and feeling low, he sent his friends to ask Jesus, "Are you the one who was to come?" Jesus sent back a very uncomplicated message. Tell John that, "the blind receive sight, the lame walk, those who have leprosy are cured, the deaf hear, the dead are raised, and the good news is preached to the poor." (Luke 7:22) The evidence of Jesus being the person John had spoken of was his life of compassion and caring for the downtrodden.

Consistent with the life of Jesus are his teachings on who shall inherit "eternal life." In Matthew 25:32-46, Jesus describes how someday all the nations will be gathered before him, and he will separate the people one from another. Eternal life is granted to those who followed the example of Jesus by feeding the hungry, giving water to the thirsty, inviting in strangers, clothing those in need, and visiting those in prison. There was no mention of one's baptism, beliefs, church attendance, or the fulfillment of any of the other multitude of religious requirements.

Over the past 20 years, I have begun to wonder if we as Christians have lost our focus. It seems as though we have been so concerned about what we are against that we have been distracted from what we should be doing on a daily basis that would please Jesus. I am becoming increasingly convinced that the life lived by Jesus, one of compassion and caring for those in need, is the model for our life and is to be our purpose. These teachings are not unlike those of the

Buddha and Confucius. I believe that if Jesus were present on earth today, he would speak out against the religious establishments of our day, especially the televangelists with their considerable wealth and control over people, a practice seemingly present in all of religion. I believe he would speak out against churches that feel they have a "lock" on the truth and church members who are judgmental and condemning of others.

While I no longer accept the Bible as the Word of God, as noted previously, the Bible has much wisdom and council for living our lives.

A few New Testament teachings regarding caring for those in need, radiating good deeds, and being generous are listed in the following chart.

Verse	Teaching
Matt 25: 32, 34, 40	All the nations will be gathered before him, and he will separate the people one from another...come, you who are blessed by my Father; take your inheritance, the kingdom prepared for you... for I was hungry and you gave me something to eat, I was thirsty and you gave me something to drink, I was a stranger and you invited me in, I needed clothes and you clothed me, I was sick and you looked after me, I was in prison and you came to visit me...**whatever you did for one of the least of these brothers of mine, you did for me.**
Ja 1:27	Religion that God our Father accepts as pure and fault-less is this: **to look after orphans and widows in their distress.**
I Tim 6: 17-18	Command those who are rich...to do good...**and to be generous** and willing to share.
I John 3: 17	If anyone has material possessions and sees his brother in need but has no pity on him, how can the love of God be in him.
Phil 2:4	Each of you should look not only to your own interests, but also to the interests of others.
Gal 6: 9-10	Let us not be weary in **doing good**...as we have opportunity, let us **do good,** to all people.
Ep 2:9	For we are God's workmanship, **created...to do good works.**
Ja 2:14	What good is it...if a man claims to have faith but has no deeds?
Ja 2:18	I will show you my faith by what I do.
Tit 3: 1-2,8	Remind the people...to be ready to do whatever is **good**, to slander no one, to be **peaceable and consid-erate**, and to **show true humility** toward all men... careful to devote themselves to doing what is good.

Verse	Teaching
I Pet 2:12	Live such good lives among the pagans that, though they accuse you of doing wrong, they **may see your good deeds and glorify God.**
II Pet 1: 5-11	Make every effort to add to your faith goodness; and to goodness, knowledge; and to knowledge, self-control; and to self-control, perseverance; and to perseverance, godliness; and to godliness, brotherly kindness; and to brotherly kindness, love. For **if you possess these qualities** in increasing measure, they will keep you from being ineffective and unproductive.
Gal 5:22	But the **fruit of the Spirit is love,** joy, peace, patience, kindness, goodness, faithfulness, gentleness, and self-control.
Phil 4: 5	Let your **gentleness be evident to all.**
Phil 4: 8	Whatever is true, whatever is noble, whatever is right, whatever is pure, whatever is lovely, whatever is ad-mirable—think about such things.
I Thes 5: 16-18	Be joyful always, pray continually, give thanks in all cir-cumstances.
Matt 19: 16-21	(Question to Jesus from the Rich young ruler): What good thing must I do to get eternal life?... (Response from Jesus): If you want to be perfect...**Sell** your posses-sions **and give to the poor.**
Mark 10: 17-21	(Question to Jesus from the Rich young ruler): What must I do to inherit eternal life? (Response from Jesus): **Sell** everything you have **and give to the poor.**
Lk 18: 18-30	(Question to Jesus from the Rich young ruler): What must I do to inherit eternal life? (Response from Jesus): **Sell** everything you have and **give to the poor.**
I Tim 6:10	For the love of money is a root of all kinds of evil.
Lk 12:48	From everyone who has been given much, much will be demanded; and from the one who has been entrusted with much, much more will be asked.

The Bible also has much to say about loving our enemies, avoiding judging others, and the need to forgive. A few New Testament teaching are listed in the following chart.

Verse	Teaching
Matt 22:36-40	Teacher, which is the greatest commandment in the Law? Jesus replied: **Love the Lord your God** with all your heart and with all your mind. This is the first and greatest commandment. And the second is like it: **Love your neighbor as yourself.** All the law and the prophets hang on these two commandments.
Jn 15: 12-13, 17	**My command is this: love each other** as I have loved you. Greater love has no one than this, that he lay down his life for his friends.... This is my command: love each other.
Ro 13: 9-10	Love your neighbor as yourself. Love does no harm to its neighbor. Therefore, **love is the fulfillment of the law**.
I Cor 13	If I speak in the tongues of humans and angels but have no love, I have become a reverberating gong or a clashing cymbal. If I have the gift of prophecy and can understand all secrets and every form of knowledge, and if I have absolute faith so as to move mountains but have no love, I am nothing. Even if I give away all that I have and surrender my body so that I may boast but have no love, I get nothing out of it. Love is always patient. Love is always kind. Love is never envious....Never does she think of self, or ever get annoyed. She never is resentful...three things remain: faith, hope, and love. But **the greatest of these is love.**
I John 4: 7-8	Dear friends, let us love one another, for love comes from God...because **God is love.**
Matt 5:43	**Love your enemies,** pray for those who persecute you.
Matt 5:7	**Blessed are the merciful,** for they will be shown mercy.
Matt 5:9	**Blessed are the peacemakers,** for they will be called children of God.

Verse	Teaching
Mat 7:1	**Do not judge**, or you too will be judged.
Luke 6:27	**Do not judge,** and you will not be judged. Do not condemn, and you will not be condemned. Forgive, and you will be forgiven.
Ep 4: 29-32	Do not let any unwholesome talk come out of your mouths, but only what is helpful for building others up...get rid of all bitterness, rage and anger...be kind and compassionate to one another, **forgiving each other**.
Col 3: 12-14	Clothe yourselves with compassion, kindness, humility, gentleness, and patience. Bear with each other and **forgive whatever grievances you may** have against one another...and over all these virtues put on love.
I Pet 3:8-9	Live in harmony with one another, be sympathetic, love as brothers, be compassionate and humble. **Do not repay evil with evil or insult** with insult but with blessing.

It seems to me that these guidelines (teachings) from the New Testament, which are consistent with the teachings of a multitude of sages and wisdom teachers, suggest what the focus of a progressive Christian should be. If the Bible is no longer accepted as the written Word of God, perhaps we should not only read and study the Bible but also look to the writings of other world religions. It is interesting to consider the Golden Rule as found in various forms in many different religions. Perhaps it can be said that it is intrinsic in all humans, since even individuals who claim to be atheists, try to follow the Golden Rule. The following are a few examples of the Golden Rule from a number of religions and ethnic groups. (*Religious Tolerance: Ontario Consultants on Religious Tolerance*)

Religion	Golden Rule Statement
Baha'i	"Lay not on any soul a load which ye would not wish to be laid upon you, and desire not for any one the things ye would not desire for yourselves." Baha'u'llah
Buddhism	"Treat not others in ways that you yourself would find hurtful." Udana-Varga 5:18
Christianity	"All things whatsoever ye would that men should do to you, do ye even so to them." Matthew 7:1
Confucianism	"Surely it is the maxim of loving-kindness: Do not unto others that you would not have them do unto you." Analects 12:2
Hinduism	This is the sum of duty; do naught onto others what you would not have them do unto you. Mahabharata 5,15,17
Islam	Not one of you truly believes until you wish for others what you wish for yourself. Hadith (Sahih Al-Bukhari)
Jainism	"One should treat all creatures in the world as one would like to be treated."—Mahavira, Sutrakritanga 1.11.33
Judaism	What is hateful to you, do not do to your neighbor. This is the whole Torah; all the rest is commentary. Go and learn it. Hillel, Talmud, Shabbath 31a
Native American	"Our fathers gave us many laws, which they had learned from their fathers. These laws were good. They told us to treat all men as they treated us; that we should never be the first to break a bargain; that it was a disgrace to tell a lie; that we should speak only the truth..." Chief Joseph, Nez Perce
Sikhism	"I am a stranger to no one; and no one is a stranger to me. Indeed, I am a friend to all." Guru Granth Sahib
Taoism	"Regard your neighbor's gain as your own gain and your neighbor's loss as your own loss." T'ai Shang Kan Ying P'ien
Zoroastrian-ism	"Do not do unto others whatever is injurious to your-self."—Shayast-na-Shayast 13.29

In addition to the Bible and the writings of other religions there are three national/international church organizations that provide direction. First, the World Council of Churches adopted the AGAPE Document. (*Alternative Globalization Addressing Peoples and Earth*, Accessed June 14, 2012) This document is a "call for love and action." They suggest that Christians have become apathetic to suffering and injustice to the "least of these among us" and those living at the margins of society. "We are tempted to give in to comfort and its empty promises when we ought to choose costly discipleship."

Second, the World Alliance of Reformed Churches adopted the Accra Confession, covenanting for justice in the economy and the earth at its 24th General Council, in Accra, Ghana, August 13, 2004. (Accessed June 14, 2012) The document lists 42 specific statements challenging Christians to follow the example and teachings of Jesus to hear the cries of the oppressed, the destitute, the poor, the exploited, the wronged, and the abused and take action to "break the chains of oppression and the yoke of injustice, and let the oppressed go free." (Isaiah 58:6)

Third, the General Assembly of the National Council of Churches of Christ in the USA adopted a "*Social Creed for the Twenty-first Century.*" (Accessed June 14, 2012) This document builds on the 1908 "Social Creed" and offers a vision of a society that shares more and consumes less, seeks compassion over suspicion and equality over domination, and finds security in joined hands rather than massed arms. They promote Isaiah's vision of a "peaceable kingdom," (Isaiah 65:23) and the vision of Jesus "that all may have life, and have it abundantly." (John 10:10)

So, as a Christian, how do I live my life with the purpose to follow the model Jesus gave us? His use of the metaphors of clothing, food, and drink are only examples and lead me to ask of myself:

1. To what extent am I assisting those in need; the homeless, the hungry, those without healthcare, those who lack opportunities, the child, the widow, the orphan, the elderly, the disabled, and others? What form should assistance take? What am I doing about poverty and income inequity?

2. To what extent am I demonstrating my love for enemies? To what extent am I demonstrating not judging those with whom I might not agree? To what extent am I demonstrating my forgiveness? What am I doing to reduce violence and promote peace?

3. What talents, gifts, and resources do I possess so I can assist and support others?

4. How do I balance my taking action to assist and support others with my own personal needs and interests?

I am reminded of the excellent statement by Martin Luther King, Jr., "Philanthropy is commendable, but it must not cause the philanthropist to overlook the circumstances of economic injustice which make philanthropy necessary." Of the 20 leading developed countries, the USA has the greatest income inequality. In the 1970's the richest 1% controlled 8% of our nation's wealth. By 2009, the richest 1% controlled 43% of our nation's wealth. In the 1950's the top 1% paid a 70-90% income tax rate, in the 1970's the top 1% paid a 50-70% income tax and by 2002 it was lowered to 35%. In 1980 the income of CEO's was 50 times that of the average worker, but by 2006 it was 300 times the average worker. I wonder if we are becoming a Plutocracy. The Bible is clear in its teachings that the rich must share what they have. (I John 3:17; I Timothy 6:17-18; Luke 12:48) I have always heard that Americans are the most generous people on Earth. Unfortunately, statistics don't support that contention. Consistent with our income inequality, of the 20 most developed nations, the USA is next to last in per capita giving to the poor.

We have the most relaxed gun laws of the 20 leading industrial nations and the highest number of deaths from guns with about 11,000 gun deaths per year. This averages out to 10.2 deaths per 100,000 population in the USA compared to .07 in Japan, .25 in United Kingdom .63 in Spain, 1.05 in Australia, 1.10 in Germany, 1.78 in Norway, 3.13 in Canada, and 3.0 in France. With just 5% of the world's population, we account for half of the world's military spending. Unfortunately, when asked about gun control, the majority of evangelicals in the USA indicated the need to have a gun to protect their religious freedom. Also, evangelicals were the demographic most supportive of the use of torture of enemies. I find both of these positions expressed by evangelicals to be contrary to the teachings and example of Jesus. Jesus said "turn your cheek" not "pull your gun." In her article, "Is Gun Ownership Christian," Lisa Miller wrote to evangelicals who argue for the right of Christians to own guns, "owning a gun is contrary to the life and teachings of Jesus. That may sound like a hard truth, but for a Christian, there's no way around it." (Miller) As stated by Anne Rice earlier, these are additional reasons why I quit being an evangelical, yet continue to be an ardent follower of Jesus.

Since the greatest sources of unnecessary human misery are economic injustice, violence, and war, in addition to volunteer work, service, and giving, I believe I also need to make judgments about whom and what to support in the public arena based upon whether or not a policy and practice benefits the disenfranchised and promotes justice and peace. Consistent with the principles of Progressive Christianity and the teachings of Jesus, some of the public policy areas I believe important are:

- Support policies that provide access to quality health care for everyone.
- Support policies that provide a "safety net" for children, the eld-

erly and disabled such as social security, Medicare, Medicaid and numerous other social services.

- Support policies that provide access to quality education and job training for all individuals.
- Support policies and practices that do not give preferential treatment to the wealthy, rather call for the wealthy to provide support for the needy which means, in part, increase taxes on higher incomes. Policies that favor the wealthy are contrary to the teachings of Jesus.
- Support policies that promote safety and security for all persons.
- Support policies that focus on rehabilitation of those that break the law.
- Do not raise barriers against individuals and activities that we personally or theologically disagree with, such as abortion, gender equality, and same sex-marriage.
- Going to war with other nations should be a last resort and only after the evidence of need is overwhelming and the nations of the world are in general agreement.
- Talk to your enemies and seek to understand them.
- Do not push your religious beliefs on others, rather, live your religious beliefs by the compassion and kindness you show towards others.
- Consistent with much of the civilized world, the American public does not need guns, except those that can be used for hunting and law enforcement. Guns kill, all too often the innocent and the poor. I see no evidence in the teaching of Jesus that we should own guns or pursue any means of violence.

Richard Stearns (2009), President of World Vision, wrote "What is the Christian faith about…what does God expect of me?" (p.1) A very powerful and challenging book calling us to love God by loving and caring for our neighbor, both those near and far, those like us and those different from us, those who are our friends and those who are enemies, and those who believe like us and those who don't. He indicates that perhaps Mohandas Gandhi said it best, "I like your Christ, I do not like your Christians. Your Christians are so unlike your Christ."

Gire (1998) proposes that since it is clear that what pleases God is our love of him and our neighbor, and that we love God by our love of others, at the end of the day as we lay in bed, we should reflect "have I loved well today? Has love been the beating heart pulsing through all my activities? Can it be heard in all my conversations? Seen in my eyes? Felt when others are in my presence? Were my decisions I made today based on my love?"

Finally, as a progressive Christian, I care about our planet. In the mid to late 1980's when we lived in Tulsa and were firmly in the conservative Christian/political point of view, we had Jim Inhofe in our home as we supported his run for a political office. While he did not win the election then, he later became the Republican Senator from Oklahoma. Now, I am stunned at what he is advocating. In 2012 he wrote, "Genesis 8:22 says that as long as the earth remains there will be seed time and harvest, cold and heat, winter and summer, day and night." He says, "my point is, God's still up there. The arrogance of people to think that we, human beings, would be able to change what he is doing in the climate is to me outrageous." (*The Greatest Hoax: How the Global Warming Conspiracy Threatens Your Future*) Inhofe believes that it is impossible that man has anything to do with global warming. He also says that the Bible warns us not to put an emphasis on the environment. He states that in Romans 1:25, it says, "'they give up the truth about God for a lie and they worship God's creation instead of God." As Inhofe claims, "when people say we should take care of the environment, they are trying to say we should worship the creation. We were reminded in the Bible that this was going to happen and sure enough it's happening." The position taken by Inhofe reminds me of the middle ages when the church claimed that the earth was flat and people were imprisoned if they disagreed with this belief. When one's interpretation of the Bible supersedes science and reason, people suffer.

Such positions, when taken by a political leader, can have extremely harmful consequences to our entire earth and all the people living on it. The future of our earth depends on a realization that climate change is happening and humans have a responsibility to care for our home, the earth that is God's creation. As I write this, where I live near Denver, Colorado, we have just set all-time records going back over 130 years for the number of days over 100, the number of days over 90, and we are experiencing a terrible drought. The sea ice in the Arctic has shrunk to the lowest level since they began collecting data. Violent storms have battered our country and wild fires have caused devastation. In 2012 the temperature on earth was the warmest since recorded history. Numerous statistics gathered from around the earth confirm the fact of global warming and humans' role in this process. Researchers from Harvard and the University of Oregon looked at global temperature over the past 11,300 years and report that the earth is "warming at an unprecedented rate." (Marcott)

While numerous conservative Christians support Inhofe's assertions, fortunately, many religious groups are beginning to recognize and accept that as part of our Christian responsibility, we should care for all of God's creation, including the earth. One example of this is the Mennonite Creation Care Network. (Accessed June 2, 2012) This organization works to encourage people to become engaged in caring for creation. Their 4 specific goals are:

1. Establish the Biblical and theological foundation for the care of God's creation.
2. Discover the ties that link all created beings to each other and to God.
3. Confess the harm we have caused the natural world and our neighbors.
4. Act faithfully to restore the earth.

Since many conservative/evangelical Christians have endorsed the Inhofe approach to the environment, a group called the Christians for Environmental Stewardship has been formed. (*Christian Ecology*, Accessed June 2, 2012) They are dedicated specifically to reaching the evangelical and conservative Christian churches with a scriptural message of environmental stewardship. They feel that God expects, even demands, that we be stewards of his creation. Every time a species goes extinct, we are defaulting on the account that God has called us to manage. They suggest we are at the crossroads, able to choose to save or to destroy. It is our choice. Christians are called to be stewards, to nurture, to protect, and to preserve God's creation.

Chapter Seventeen

CONCLUDING COMMENTS

Living a progressive Christian life is to make a vital effort to focus one's life on humanity's needs and rebuff the radical individualism so ubiquitous in our culture and "popular" Christianity. It rejects the focus in "popular" Christianity of "Me-ism," the self-centered focus on our personal salvation that God is personally taking care of me, will heal me when I'm sick, wants me to be wealthy, wants everything wonderful for me including heaven when I die, and that Christianity is all about believing the right things. Progressive Christianity emphasizes personal transformation with social consciousness. It means being a follower of the life and teachings of Jesus, being passionate about the things Jesus was passionate about, taking action. It challenges us to do the hard things; to confront the political, religious, economic, and social domination systems of our culture. It emphasizes a focus on others, especially those disenfranchised because of race/ethnicity, gender, class, sexual orientation, poverty, homelessness, religion, and diverse beliefs. It calls us to do something about the needs of the world and the environment; not just pray about them. It calls on us to be less dogmatic in our beliefs and more tolerant and accepting of those different from ourselves; to be open to the wisdom of other traditions; it calls us to be peacemakers. It calls on us to make a difference, to engage in our community. At the end of the day it calls us to reflect on our life as noted by Socrates and consider the question, "How well have I done the work of Christmas today? How well have I loved today?" As stated in the prayer of St. Francis, "Lord make me an instrument of your peace."

ACKNOWLEDGEMENTS

This book would not have happened without the influence, support, and encouragement of many. I am so appreciative of the "Grace group" in Flagstaff, AZ; Kent and Joyce Christiansen, Lew and Julie Hastings, Perry and Yvonne Shilling, Steve and Els Messenger, Al and Lynn Overend, Roger and Jane Holden, Larry and Wanda Agenbroad, and Brad and Peggy Leslie. We generally met twice monthly from 1995 until 2008 when I retired from teaching at NAU and moved to Colorado. We read, studied, explored, and considered various theological issues and ideas. Our candid, open, and deep discussions helped me to honestly confront my narrow and fundamentalist view and made a significant impact on my "letting go" of some theological views and accepting others.

I am also so thankful that when we moved to Colorado, we found two other couples seeking to examine their religions views. My spiritual and theological explorations continued with Steve and Leah Nelson and Don and Judy Engelstead as again we read, studied, discussed, and attended lectures, seminars, and went on a retreat together. What a joy it has been to have as good friends, those who are not satisfied with the status quo of their theological beliefs, and are willing to examine the core of what they believe. Confronting one's doubts and deepest concerns is not an easy task and is less painful if done with others you trust. Thanks to Steve, Leah, Don, and Judy for not only reading my writings and offering comments, but also encouraging me to put my writings into a book. Creating a book was not my original intent.

I am thankful to Paul Evanson from the Concordia College Foundations Office, my undergraduate alma mater. We had a number of theological discussions and he recommended *The Heart of Christianity* written by Concordia classmate and theologian Marcus Borg. This book so clearly outlined what I had been feeling and thinking about for many years and helped me to begin to put together my beliefs into a form that made sense to me.

Thanks to my wife, Donna, two children, Tim and Debbie, and granddaughter Brooke for reading my manuscript and making suggestions.. Thanks to my older brother, Don, who spent his life's work as a caring, compassionate pastor. We shared many emails and conversations relative to our upbringing and theological journeys as adults and I always appreciated his perspective and willingness to candidly share. As I understand what it is to live a progressive Christian life, Don exemplified it. While I have written about progressive Christianity, I find it much harder to live it. Thanks to Dr. Eleanor Hubbard who also read and made excellent suggestions. Thanks to my current pastor, Dr. Charisa Hunter-Crump who challenges me with her insights and sermons. Finally, thanks to Pam McKinnie for editing and putting the text into a format for publishing as a paperback as well as an EBook.

SOURCES AND RESOURCES

Adams, Marc. *The Preacher's Son*. Window Books, 1996.

Armstrong, Karen. *A History of God*. New York: Ballantine Books, 1993.

_____. *The Battle for God*. New York: Alfred A. Knopf, 2000.

_____. *The Case for God*. New York: Anchor Books, 2009.

Assembly of God. "The Inerrancy of Scriptures."http://ag.org/top/Beliefs/Position_Papers/pp_downloads/pp_4175_inerrancy.pdf. (Accessed October 4, 2011).

_____. "Our 16 Fundamental Truths."http://ag.org/top/Beliefs/Statement_of_Fundamental_Truths/sft_full.cfm#1. (Accessed October 4, 2011).

Baker, Brian. *Nonsense From the Bible*. Austrailia: Self Published as in E-Book, 2012.

Barr, Navada. *Seeking Enlightenment Hat by Hat: A Skeptic's Path to Religion*. New York: G. P. Putnam's Sons, 2003.

Bawer, Bruce. *Stealing Jesus: How Fundamentalism Betrays Christianity*. New York: Three Rivers Press, 1997.

Bonhoeffer, Dietrich. *Letters and Papers from Prison*. Edited by Eberhard Bethge. New York: Macmillion, 1997.

Borg, Marcus. *The Heart of Christianity: Rediscovering a Life of Faith*. New York: HarperCollins Publishers, 2003.

_____. *Jesus: Uncovering the Life, Teachings, and Relevance of a Religious Revolutionary*. New York: HarperCollins Publishers, 2006.

_____. *Putting Away Childish Things: A tale of modern faith*. New York: HarperCollins Publishers, 2010.

_____. *Speaking Christian*. New York: HarperCollins Publishers, 2011.

Bourgeault, Cynthia. *The Wisdom of Jesus: A New Perspective on Christ and His Message.* Boston: Shambhala, 2008.

Braestrup, Kate. *Here if You Need Me.* New York: Back Bay Book, 2007.

Bronner, Ethan. "Gay Marriage Gains Backer as Major Foe Revises Views." *New York Times.* June 6, 2012. http://www.nytimes.com /2012/06/23/us/david-blankenhorn-drops-opposition-to-gay-marriage.html. (Accessed June 24, 2012).

Bruni, Frank. "Genetic or Not, Gay Won't Go Away." *New York Times.* January 28, 2012.

Butler Bass, Diana. *Christianity After Religion: The End of the Church and the Birth of a New Spiritual Awakening.* New York: HarperCollins Publishers, 2012.

Carey, Benedict. "Psychiatry Giant Sorry for Backing Gay 'Cure.'" *New York Times.* May 18, 2012. http://www.nytimes.com/ 2012/05/19/health/dr-robert-l-spitzer-noted-psychiatrist-apol-ogizes-for-study-on-gay-cure.html?_r=1&hp. (Accessed May 19, 2012).

Christian Ecology. "A Scriptural Call for Environmental Steward-ship." http://www.christianecology.org/Stewardship.html. (Ac-cessed June 2, 2012).

Claiborne, Shane. *The Irresistible Revolution: Living as an Ordinary Radical.* Grand Rapids: Zondervan, 2006.

Cobb, John. Ed. *Progressive Christians Speak.* Louisville: Westminster John Knox Press, 2003.

Collins, Francis. *The Language of God.* New York: Free Press, 2006.

Community Bible Church. "Statement of Beliefs." http://www. montecbc.com/beliefs-vision/. (Accessed February 28, 2012).

Crossan, John Dominic and Reed, Jonathan. *Excavating Jesus: Beneath the Stones, Behind the Texts.* New York: HarperCollins Publishers, 2001.

Danforth, John. *Faith and Politics.* New York: Viking Press, 2006.

Dawkins, Richard. *The God Delusion.* New York: First Mariner Books, 2008.

Dorn, Paul. "Really? Did God say that?" *Daily Camera.* January 29, 2012. http://www.dailycamera.com/ci_19837244. (Accessed April 9, 2012).

Dorn, Paul. "Did God Say that? Part 2" *Daily Camera.* March 8, 2012. www.dailycamera.com/guestopinion/ci_20342256/guest-commentary-did-god-say-that-part-2 (Accessed April 9, 2012).

Dreyfus, Hubert and Kelly, Sean. *All Things Shining.* New York: Free Press, 2011.

Eckholm, Erik. "Preaching Virtue of Spanking, Even as Deaths Fuel Debate." *New York Times.* November 6, 2011. http://www. nytimes.com/2011/11/07/us/deaths-put-focus-on-pastors-advocacy-of-spanking.html?pagewanted=1&_r=0. (Accessed November 9, 2011).

Ehrman, Bart. *The New Testament: A Historical Introduction to the Early Christian Writings.* New York: Oxford University Press, 2011.

_____. *After the New Testament: The Writings of the Apostolic Fathers.* New York: HarperCollins Publishers, 2005.

_____. *Misquoting Jesus: The Story Behind who Changed the Bible and Why.* New York: HarperCollins Publishers, 2007.

_____. *God's Problem: How the Bible Fails to Answer our Most Important Question, Why we Suffer.* New York: HarperCollins Publishers, 2008.

_____. *Jesus, Interrupted: Revealing the Hidden Contradictions in the Bible.* New York: HarperCollins Publishers, 2009.

Evangelical Free Church. "Statement of Faith."http://www.efca .org/about-efca/statement-faith. (Accessed July 25, 2012).

Farley, Wendy. *Gathering Those Driven Away.* Louisville: Westminster John Knox Press, 2011.

Fox, Richard. *Reinhold Niebuhr: A Biography.* New York: Pantheon Books, 1985.

____. *A History of Jesus in America: Personal Savior, Cultural Hero, National Obsession.* New York: HarperCollins Publishers, 2004.

Gire, Ken. *The Reflective Life.* Colorado Springs: Chariot Victor Publishing, 1998.

Girzone, Joseph. *Joshua.* New York: Scribner Paperback, 1987.

_____. *A Portrait of Jesus.* New York: Image Books, 1998.

Gomes, Peter. *The Scandalous Gospel of Jesus.* New York: HarperCollins Publishers, 2007.

Gulley, Philip and Mulholland, James. *If Grace is True: Why God will Save Every Person.* New York: HarperCollins Publishers, 2003.

_____. *If God is Love: Rediscovering Grace in an Ungracious World.* New York: HarperCollins Publishers, 2004.

Harris, Sam. *Letter to a Christian Nation.* New York: Vintage Books, 2008.

Haught, James A., *2000 Years of Disbelief,* New York: Prometheus, 1996.

Hedges, Chris. *American Fascists: The Christian Right and the War on America.* New York: Simon & Schuster, 2006.

Hosseini, Khaled. *The Kite Runner.* New York: Riverhead Books, 2003.

_____. *A Thousand Splendid Suns.* New York: Riverhead Books, 2007.

Houreld, Katharine. "African Children Denounced As 'Witches' By Christian Pastors." *Huffington Post.* October 18, 2009. http://www.huffingtonpost.com/2009/10/18/african-children-denounce_n_324943.html. (Accessed October 20, 2009).

Hubbard, Eleanor, and Whitley, Cameron. Editors. *Trans-Kin: A Guide for Family & Friends of Transgender People.* Boulder: Boulder Press, 2012.

Idliby, Ranya, Oliver, Suzanne, and Warner, Priscilla. *The Faith Club.*

New York: Free Press, 2006.

Ingersoll, Robert G. *The Works of Ingersoll.* New York: Dresden, 1901.

Jackson, David. "Many Southern Republicans say Obama is Muslim." *USA Today.* March 12, 2012. http://content.usatoday.com/communities/theoval/post/2012/03/many-southern-gopers-say-obama-is-muslim/1. (Accessed, March 12, 2012).

Jacobsen, Douglas, and Sawatsky, Rodney. *Gracious Christianity.* Grand Rapids: Baker Academic, 2006.

Jensen, Robert. *All my Bones Shake: Seeking a Progressive Path to the Prophetic Voice.* Brooklyn: Soft Skull Press, 2009.

Johnson, Paul. *A History of the Jews.* New York: Harper Perennial, 1987.

Kaplan, Rebecca. "Santorum: Obama College Plan Aimed at Indoctrination." *National Journal.* February 23, 2012. http://www.nationaljournal.com/2012-presidential-campaign/santorum-obama-college-plan-aimed-at-indoctrination—20120223. (Accessed March 12, 2012).

Keating, Peter. "The Right Calls Obama Hitler." *New Yorker.* October 14, 2009. http://nymag.com/daily/intel/2009/10/the_right_calls_obama_hitler_w.html. (Accessed October 21, 2009).

Keating, Thomas. *Intimacy with God: An Introduction to Centering Prayer.* New York: A Crossroad book, 2009.

Kidd, Sue Monk. *The Dance of the Dissident Daughter.* New York: HarperCollins, 1996.

Kingsolver, Barbara. *The Poisonwood Bible.* New York: HarperCollins, 1998.

Knitter, Paul. *Without Buddha I Could Not Be a Christian.* Oxford: Oneworld Publications, 2009.

Krasny, Michael. *Spiritual Envy.* Novato: New World Library, 2010.

Kraybill, Donald, Nolt, Steven, and Weaver-Zercher, David. *Amish Grace: How Forgiveness Transcended Tragedy.* San Francisco: Jossey-

Bass Publisher, 2007.

Kuo, David. *Tempting Faith*. New York: Free Press, 2006.

Lamb, David. *God Behaving Badly: Is the God of the Old Testament Angry, Sexist and Racist?*. Downers Grove: InterVarsity Press, 2011.

Lamott, Anne. *Grace Eventually: Thoughts on Faith*. New York: Riverhead Books, 2007.

Lerner, Michael. *The Left Hand of God*. New York: HarperCollins Publishers, 2006.

Lindsey, Hal. *The Late Great Planet Earth*. Grand Rapids: Zondervan Press, 1970.

Marcott, Shaun, et al. "A Reconstruction of Regional and Global Temperatures for the Past 11,300 Years." *Science*. March 8, 2013. http://www.sciencemag.org/content/339/6124/1198/suppl/DC1.

McCowan, Karen. "Couple's children become wards of the state." *The Register-Guard*. April 17, 2012. http://projects.registerguard.com/web/newslocalnews/27925273-41/bellew-state-russel-care-medical.html.csp. (Accessed June 2, 2012).

McLaren, Brian. *Generous Orthodoxy*. Grand Rapids: Youth Specialties, 2004.

Meacham, Jon "Rethinking Heaven." *Time*. April 16, 2012.

Mesle, Robert. *Process Theology*. St. Louis: Chalice Press, 1993.

Mennonite Creation Care Network. http://www.mennocreationcare.org/. (Accessed June 2, 2012).

Meyers, Robin. *Saving Jesus from the Church*. New York: HarperCollins Publishers, 2009.

_____. *The Underground Church*. San Francisco: Jossey-Bass, 2012.

Miller, Lisa. "For Santorums, personal tragedy turned political." *The Washington Post*. January 20, 2012. http://www.washingtonpost.com/national/on-faith/personal-tragedy-becomes-political-pawn/2012/01/19/gIQA75LdDQ_story.html. (Accessed March

21, 2012).

_____. "Is Gun Ownership Christian?" *The Washington Post.* January 25, 2013. http://www.washingtonpost.com/local/is-gun-owner-ship-christian/2013/01/25/c7afe7fe-6724-11e2-93e1-475791032daf_story.html. (Accessed March 26, 2013).

Moore, Thomas. *Care of the Soul.* New York: HarperCollins Publishers, 1992.

_____. *The Soul's Religion.* New York: HarperCollins Publishers, 2002.

Moran, Caitlin. *How to be a Woman.* London: Ebury Press, 2011.

Moreland, J. P. *Love Your God with all Your Mind: The role of Reason in the Life of the Soul.* Colorado Springs: NavPress, 1997.

National Council of Churches USA and Church World Service. "A Social Creed for the 21st Century." November 7, 2007. http://www.ncccusa.org/news/ga2007.socialcreed.html. (Accessed June 14, 2012).

Nolan, Albert. *Jesus Before Christianity.* Maryknoll: Orbis Books, 1992.

O'Murchu, Diarmuid. *Adult Faith: Growing in Wisdom and Understanding.* Maryknoll: Orbis Books, 2010.

Pagels, Elaine. *Revelations: Visions, Prophecy, & Politics.* New York: Viking Press, 2012.

Palmer, Parker. T*he Promise of Paradox: A Celebration of Contradictions in the Christian Life.* San Francisco: Jossey-Bass, 2008.

"Pastor Dennis Terry Introduces Rick Santorum, Tells Non-Christians And Liberals To Get Out" *Huffington Post Video.* March 19, 2012. http://www.huffingtonpost.com/2012/03/19/dennis-terry-rick-santorum_n_1364414.html. (Accessed March 19, 2012).

Pearce, C. S. *This we Believe: The Christian Case for Gay Civil Rights.* Claremont: Pomona Press, 2012.

Pearson, Carlton. *God is not a Christian, nor a Jew, Muslim, Hindu....*

New York: Atria Books, 2010.

Peck, M. Scott. *The Different Drum: Community Making and Peace.* New York: Touchstone, 1987.

Peters, Ralph. *Behond Terror.* Mechanicsburg, PA.: Stackpole Books. 2002.

Peters, Rebecca Todd. T*o Do Justice: A Guide for Progressive Christians.* London: Westminster John Knox Press, 2008.

Peterson, Brenda. *I Want to be Left Behind.* Cambridge: Da Capo Press. 2008.

Pew Forum on Religion & Public Life. "Global Christianity: A Report on the Size and Distribution of the World's Christian Population." December 19, 2011. http://www.pewforum.org/ Christian/Global-Christianity-worlds-christian-population.aspx. (Accessed June 30, 2012).

Pew Forum on Religion & Public Life. "'Nones' on the Rise" October 9, 2012. http://www.pewforum.org/Unaffiliated/nones-on-the-rise.aspx. (Accessed October 23, 2012).

Phillips, Kevin. *American Theocracy.* New York: Penguin Books, 2006.

Piatt, Christian. "Death by Faith Healing: A Church-State Separation Dilemma." *Sojourners.* April 18, 2012. http://sojo.net/ blogs/2012/04/18/death-faith-healing-church-state-separation-dilemma. (Accessed June 2, 2012).

PoliGu.com. "Rick Santorum on Abortion." January 4, 2012. http://www.thepoliticalguide.com/Profiles/Senate/Pennsylvania/Rick_Santorum/Views/Abortion/. (Accessed March 20, 2012).

Pond, Lauren. "Why I watched a Snake Handling Pastor die for his Faith." *The Washington Post.* May 31, 2012. http://www.washingtonpost.com/lifestyle/style/why-i-watched-a-snake-handling-pastor-die-for-his-faith/2012/05/31/gJQA3fRP5U_story.html?h pid=z3. (Accessed June 1, 2012).

Progressive Christianity. "The Phoenix Affirmations." http://progressivechristianity.org/resources/the-phoenix-affirmations-full-version/. (Accessed October 25, 2012).

Prothero, Stephen. *American Jesus: How the Son of God became a National Icon.* New York: Farrar, Straus and Giroux, 2003.

Ranke-Heinemann, Uta. *Putting Away Childish Things.* New York: HarperCollins Publishers,1994.

Religious Tolerance: Ontario Consultants on Religious Tolerance. "Shared Belief in the Golden Rule." http://www.religioustolerance.org/reciproc.htm. (Accessed May 22, 2012).

Richo, David. *How to be an Adult in Faith and Spirituality.* New York: Paulist Press, 2011.

Riley, Gregory. *One Jesus, Many Christ's.* New York: HarperCollins Publishers, 1998.

Robinson, John. *Honest to God.* London: Westminster John Knox Press, 1963.

Rohr, Richard. *The Naked Now: Learning to see as the Mystics see.* New York: A Crossroad Book, 2009.

Salem Witch Trials. http://en.wikipedia.org/wiki/Salem_witch_trials. (Accessed November 15, 2009).

Sanford, Charles. *The Religious Life of Thomas Jefferson.* Charlottesville: University of Virginia Press, 1995.

Schaeffer, Frank. *Crazy for God: How I grew up as One of the Elect, Helped found the Religious Right, and Lived to take it all Back.* New York: Carroll & Graf Publishers, 2007.

Seibert, Eric, *Disturbing Divine Behavior: Troubling Old Testament Images of God.* Minneapolis: Fortress Press, 2009.

Sheldon, Charles. *In His Steps.* Old Tappan: Fleming Revell Company. 1975.

Silverman, Herb. *God and Smallpox.* http://www.lowcountryhumanists.org/SEPS/sep-2001-11.html. (Accessed January 17, 2013).

Smith, Christian. *The Bible Made Impossible*. Grand Rapids: Brazos Press, 2011.

Sommer, Joseph. *Violence and the Biblical God*. http://www.humanism-byjoe.co/violence-and-the-Biblical-god/. (Accessed June 30, 2012).

Spong, John Shelby. *The Sins of Scripture*. New York: HarperCollins Publishers, 2005.

_____. *Jesus for the Non-Religious*. New York: HarperCollins Publishers, 2007.

_____. *Eternal Life: A New Vision*. New York: HarperCollins Publishers, 2009.

Stearns, Richard. *The Hole in our Gospel*. Nashville: Thomas Nelson, 2009.

Sumrall, Lester. *I Predict 2000 AD*. Sumrall Press, 1987.

Taylor, Daniel. *The Myth of Certainty: The Reflective Christian and the Risk of Commitment*. Waco: Word Books Publisher, 1986.

Taylor, John. *The Literal Meaning of Genesis*. New York: Newman Press, 1982.

"Thousand Protest Pastor Charles Worley Who Preached Putting Gays And Lesbians In Electrified Pen." *Huffington Post Video*. http://www.huffingtonpost.com/2012/05/27/protesters-denounce-minis_n_1549339.html. (Accessed June 8, 2012).

Thrasher, J. B. "Slavery: A Divine Institution." November 5, 1860. http://www.archive.org/stream/slaverydivineins00thra/slavery-divineins00thra_djvu.txt. (Accessed March 12, 2012).

Tickle, Phyllis. *The Great Emergence: How Christianity is Changing and Why*. Grand Rapids: Baker Books, 2008.

Tippett, Krista. *Speaking Faith*. New York: Viking. 2007.

Wallis, Jim. *Rediscovering Values*. New York: Simon & Schuster, 2010.

Walsh, Michael. *The Triumph of the Meek: Why Early Christianity Succeeded*. San Francisco: Harper & Row Publishers, 1986.

Whisenaut, Edgar. *88 Reasons Why the Rapture Will be in 1988*. Portland: Agape' Books, 1988.

Wheaton College. "Statement of Faith." http://wheaton.edu/About-Wheaton/Statement-of-Faith-and-Educational-Purpose. (Accessed July 25, 2012).

White, L. Michael. *From Jesus to Christianity*. New York: HarperCollins Publishers, 2004.

World Alliance of Reformed Churches. "Covenanting for Justice in the Economy and the Earth." July 30, 2004. http://warc.jalb.de/warcajsp/news_file/The_Accra_Confession_English.pdf. (Accessed June 14, 2012).

World Council of Churches. "A Call to Love and Action." February 14, 2006. http://www.oikoumene.org/en/resources/documents/assembly/porto-alegre-2006/3-preparatory-and-background-documents/alternative-globalization-addressing-people-and-earth-agape.html. (Accessed June 14, 2012).

Yancey, Phillip. *The Jesus I Never Knew*. Grand Rapids: Zondervan Publishing, 1995.

_____. *What's so Amazing about Grace?*. Grand Rapids: Zondervan Publishing, 1997.

_____. *Reaching for the Invisible God*. Grand Rapids: Zondervan Publishing, 2000.

_____. *Soul Survivor: How my Faith Survived the Church*. New York: Doubleday, 2001.

Young, William. *The Shack*. Los Angeles: Windblown Media, 2007.

ABOUT THE AUTHOR

Paul Brynteson was born and raised in the home of an evangelical/Pentecostal pastor. After completing a doctoral degree, he began a 40 year career (1968-2008) teaching at 4 universities in South Dakota, Arkansas, Arizona, and Oklahoma, including Oral Roberts University where he was a faculty member, department chair, and dean of a college. At age 45, after 14 years at ORU, he left discouraged and disappointed by what he had seen and experienced in evangelical/fundamentalist settings. Over the next 20 years he engaged in a serious theological journey which eventually involved leaving his Christian fundamentalism behind and adopting a more progressive, tolerant, and inclusive view of Christianity. This book is the result of that journey. He resides in Colorado with his wife of over 50 years.